THE ART OF THE
92 COUNTY WALK

Sculptures by David Jemerson Young and Jeff Laramore of 2nd Globe

Photographed by Garry Chilluffo

THE INDIANA STATE MUSEUM

Giving History Shape

92

THE ART OF THE
92 COUNTY WALK

THE INDIANA STATE MUSEUM
Giving History Shape

Sculpture photography by Garry Chilluffo
Text and book and jacket design by Young & Laramore Advertising
First published in America in 2003 by The Indiana State Museum Foundation

Text © 2003 Indiana State Museum Foundation
Illustrations © 2001 2nd Globe
Sculpture photography © 2003 Garry Chilluffo
Museum building photography © Jeff Goldberg/Esto

Library of Congress Control Number: 2003107374

ISBN 0-972-3879-1-9

Published by:
Indiana State Museum Foundation
650 West Washington Street
Indianapolis, IN 46204, USA

Printed in Hong Kong

The community of Indiana requires a central gathering place, where people from across the state may meet as one family to celebrate their rich heritage. Today, that place is the Indiana State Museum: conceived by Indiana dreamers, crafted by Indiana artisans and constructed from Indiana limestone. The museum and its 92 County Walk sculptures reflect the stories, lives and dreams of all Hoosiers, showcasing the rich tapestry of Hoosier diversity from Gary, to Evansville, to Angola, to Jeffersonville. These grounds do not simply preserve Indiana history—they celebrate what it means to be a Hoosier.

Frank O'Bannon
Forty-Seventh Governor of Indiana

FOREWORD

We are a gathered people. We came from all over to form a state named Indiana—and in doing so, we created a distinct being called a "Hoosier." Our distinctness has been formed by ancestral cultures, land conditions, sociological forces and technological advancements. To know ourselves, we must understand these influences. This exploration, in itself, is a continuous treasure hunt for identity and understanding. Amidst our journey, we find that we are not nomads, but people of a place: connected with each other, our times and our location.

Our story is that of a common cloth, woven from a variety of unique threads. As Hoosiers began organizing into communities, our signature as a state was written by the interaction between individuals and their places—creating events, habits and objects that we now gather together and call our history. The Indiana State Museum and its 92 county sculptures reflect a people united by common conditions.

Much of the Indiana State Museum, and a majority of its 92 county sculptures, is constructed from native Indiana limestone. This choice of material seems exceedingly apt, not simply because the stone is one of our state's most identifiable natural resources, but due to the nature of the material itself. Composed of the skeletons and shells of ancient organisms, limestone carries within it the evidence of innumerable past lives. Like the very stone that composes its walls, our Indiana State Museum reveals a plethora of distinct personalities, united by community and preserved beautifully for the generations to come.

Judy O'Bannon
First Lady of Indiana
May 1, 2003

Upon their first approach to the Indiana State Museum, visitors are dazzled by a dramatic building of monumental proportions. As they draw nearer, they are further engaged by a series of human-scaled sculptures integrated into the building's exterior—which use a variety of art techniques to narrate stories about the Hoosier State's 92 counties. Since the museum's opening in May 2002, this unique merger of art and architecture has been known as the 92 County Walk.

The origins of the Indiana State Museum itself date from 1862, when State Librarian Robert Delos Brown began assembling a collection of curiosities. Seven years later, the Indiana General Assembly recognized Brown's collection, and directed the state's geologist to add to it. The growing collection was moved to the Indiana State House in 1888—and rested there until 1967, when Governor Matthew E. Welsh arranged for the museum's relocation to Indianapolis' recently vacated City Hall. There, at the corner of Alabama and Ohio streets, the museum continued its mission of collecting, preserving, interpreting and sharing Indiana's history.

Throughout the late 1990s, Governor Frank O'Bannon had advocated the construction of a new museum in Indianapolis' White River State Park. In 1998, the Indiana State Office Building Commission awarded a museum building contract to the Indianapolis-based firm of Ratio Architects, Inc.

As the building commission's executive director, Susan Williams wanted a building about and for the people of Indiana. The design that Ratio produced exceeded her expectations. Ratio's architects, led by principal architect William Browne, Jr., AIA, envisioned the building's exterior as an exhibit in itself, capable of teaching passers-by about Indiana's rich history even after museum hours. To create a structure that would convey Indiana's essence, Ratio asked prominent state historians to identify defining personality characteristics of Hoosiers. The building designs that resulted reflect those conversations. The simple surface of the building's south side reflects the level lawn that leads to the museum's front door, representing the state's conservative, grounded and solid attitude. The building's north face, however, explodes into exuberant angles and individual massings—presenting the Hoosier character's spirited, contrary side.

To add to their silent narration, Ratio assembled a palate of building materials that are native to the state, ranging from the obvious limestone to such less-expected materials as sandstone (quarried in Parke County), stainless steel (developed circa 1911 in Howard County) and glass (reflecting the state's glassmaking heritage).

Wishing to establish connections with visitors from around the entire state, Williams and Browne decided that art should be created to represent each of Indiana's 92 counties. Browne turned to 2nd Globe—an Indianapolis-based company organized around artists/designers David Jemerson Young and Jeff Laramore, whose philosophy of creating narrative art with a specific public purpose suited the 92-county artwork concept perfectly.

After several discussions concerning the integration of art and architecture, 2nd Globe and Ratio determined that the 92 county-related sculptures would work in harmony with the building's design to narrate the stories of the counties' famous natives, their historically significant events, or their economic contributions.

The museum's project team solicited input from many sources, putting out calls to county commissioners, historical societies, and community foundations—who responded by suggesting points of distinction about the different counties. Once a list of county characteristics had been compiled, facts were checked for accuracy by the museum staff. When designing the area's sculpture, the artists chose the most visually interesting elements from each county. In most cases, two or more claims to regional fame were interwoven. This layering of influences was designed to engage visitors in a discovery process and to reward them on each new trip to the museum.

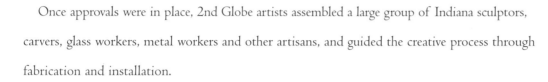

Once approvals were in place, 2nd Globe artists assembled a large group of Indiana sculptors, carvers, glass workers, metal workers and other artisans, and guided the creative process through fabrication and installation.

Meanwhile, Ratio and numerous contractors worked on the building's structure, breaking ground and building on the south side of Indianapolis' Central Canal. When completed, the innovative lines of Ratio's building design blended seamlessly with the county sculptures, in what became known collectively as the 92 County Walk. Reflecting the museum's core mission, the Walk informs, educates and engages visitors. Far more than just an entertaining experience, it stands as a consistent, unified vision; a true blend of art and architecture that shows the state its own cultural and historic roots—and provides Hoosiers with a strengthened sense of place and pride.

A patina on the bronze has made this sculpture turn green, contributing to the piece's organic feel.

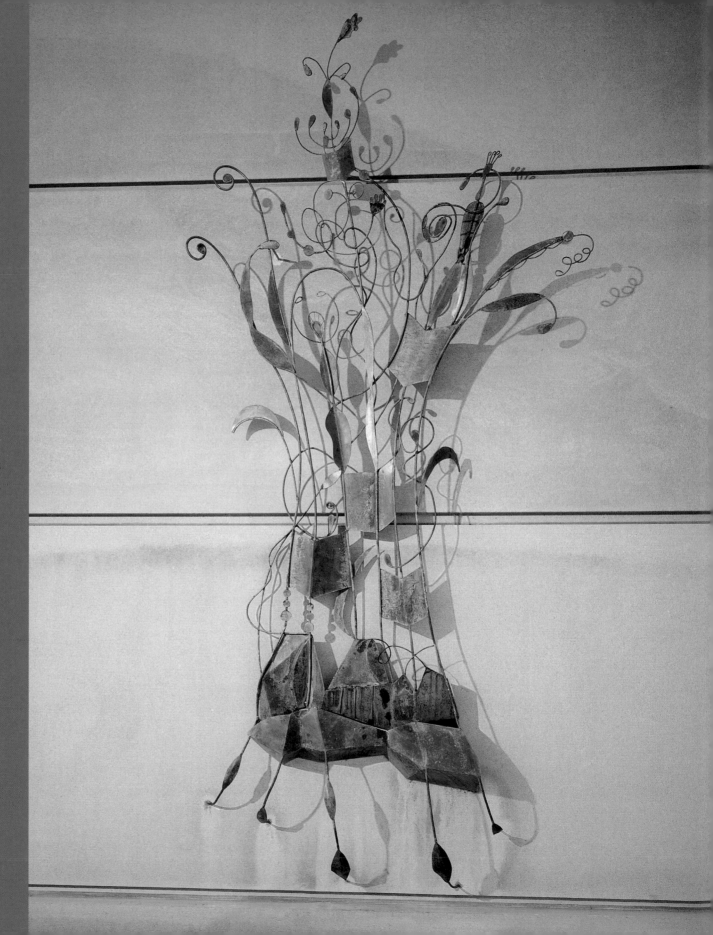

ADAMS COUNTY

Organized: 1835
Named for: John Quincy Adams
Major cities and towns: Decatur, Berne, Geneva, Monroe

■ Out of forest and swampland, a rustic cabin rises organically, resembling an exotic plant with books for leaves. This piece depicts the self-designed home of writer/naturalist Gene Stratton-Porter, who lived and worked near the 13,000-acre Limberlost Swamp from 1895 to 1913. In her books *Freckles, A Girl of the Limberlost* and other classic texts—many of which were adapted into films— Stratton-Porter shared tales deeply rooted in the natural beauty of Adams County.

Following her marriage and the birth of her daughter, Gene Stratton-Porter and her husband Charles built a 14-room home (now a state historic site) in the Adams County town of Geneva. Here, she studied the Limberlost Swamp's plant and animal life, incorporating both into her writings.

ARTIST'S NOTES

Allen County's piece contains the camouflaged form of a Native American archer, drawing his bowstring taut.

ALLEN COUNTY

Organized: 1835
Named for: John Allen
Major cities and towns: Fort Wayne, New Haven

■ As the timbers of a fort are pelted with a hail of arrows, a camouflaged archer in this piece symbolizes Allen County's long history of conflict between the French, British and American settlers and Native Americans. In 1794, following a series of brutal battles,

LARAMORE

General Anthony Wayne built a stockade here after defeating the Miami Confederation of Native Americans. A later fort, built nearby in 1800, withstood siege during the War of 1812.

■ Elsewhere in the structure, viewers may glimpse a stylized apple tree—a tribute to Johnny Appleseed, né John Chapman. Chapman, a Swedenborgian religious convert, traveled much of the Midwestern wilderness on foot during the 1800s, planting apple seedlings in strategically selected clearings. He died of pneumonia in Allen County in 1845 and was buried alongside the St. Joseph River.

MATERIALS USED:
Cast Glass, Bronze, Steel

ARTIST'S NOTES

This 40" stainless steel crankshaft was constructed by an actual machinist. Its dimensions are proportionate to the steeple of Columbus' North Christian Church.

BARTHOLOMEW COUNTY

Organized: 1821
Named for: Joseph Bartholomew
Major cities and towns: Columbus, Hope, Elizabethtown

■ This abstract engine crankshaft acknowledges the Cummins Engine Company, a longtime Bartholomew County employer. Simultaneously, exhaust pipes on the structure's side pay tribute to another local auto parts manufacturer, Arvin Industries. A narrow spire atop the piece's crest mimics the steeple of Columbus' North Christian Church, erected in 1964 by architect Eero Saarinen. Columbus, the county seat, boasts a wealth of world-renowned, architecturally significant structures—the result of an initiative begun in 1942 by Cummins chairperson J. Irwin Miller, an admirer of modernist architecture. The enterprise continues today, a fortunate convergence of industry and art.

Jemerson

Columbus contains structures designed by such highly regarded architects as Eliel Saarinen, Harry Weese, Richard Meier, Eero Saarinen and I. M. Pei.

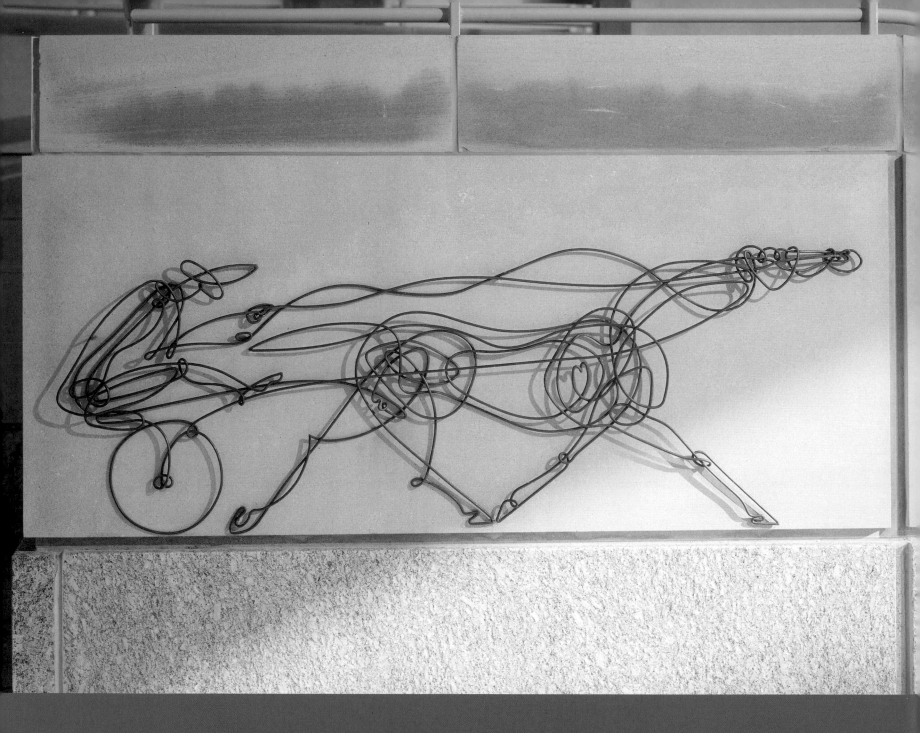

ARTIST'S NOTES

Originally sketched as a continuous line, this sculpture is constructed from lengths of 1/4" bronze rod. A viewer may begin at any point on the piece and trace around it, eventually arriving back where he or she started—duplicating the circuitous nature of a horse race itself.

BENTON COUNTY

Organized: 1840
Named for: Thomas Hart Benton
Major cities and towns: Fowler, Oxford, Otterbein, Boswell

■ A determined harness racer urges his horse forward in this sinuous, fluid form. The horse, in this case, represents Dan Patch, a trotter foaled in the Benton County town of Oxford in 1896. In 1905, at a racetrack in Lexington, Kentucky, Dan Patch ran a mile in 1:55.25, a feat that earned him world-wide fame and stood as a world record until 1938. After he achieved celebrity status, Dan Patch's image was used to sell products ranging from cigars to washing machines to automobiles. Years after his death, his reputation was still strong enough to make him the subject of a 1949 motion picture, *The Great Dan Patch.*

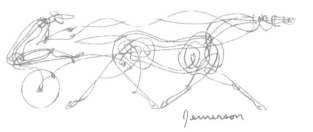

DAN PATCH

A native of Oxford, Indiana, Dan Patch ran his first harness race on August 30, 1900, in the nearby Benton County town of Boswell. In a career spanning almost ten years, Dan Patch never lost a race. By 1902, he ruled his sport so convincingly that owners refused to race their horses against him. Instead, track owners drew crowds by featuring Dan Patch alone, running against the clock in exhibitions. At the end of 1902, he was sold to a Minnesotan owner for the then-remarkable sum of $60,000. He died of an enlarged heart on July 11, 1916.

ARTIST'S NOTES

The stylized gas flame is crafted from hand-colored blue glass.

BLACKFORD COUNTY

Organized: 1838
Named for: Isaac Blackford
Major cities and towns: Hartford City, Montpelier

■ The vibrant blue flame of this piece commemorates Blackford County's illustrious history of glass making. Upon the discovery of natural gas and oil here in the 1880s, many glass factories moved to Blackford County, using the gas as an inexpensive, efficient means for melting. The arrival of these businesses and others contributed to rapid expansion throughout the county. The town of Montpelier, which numbered around 900 people when oil was discovered there in 1887, had ballooned to a population of nearly 5,000 by 1896 and was popularly known as "Oil City."

LARAMORE

At the peak of Indiana's gas boom, county seat Hartford City was home to 11 different glass companies.

ARTIST'S NOTES

Atop one column, a small bronze ball serves as a head, transforming the pillar into a whimsical hula-hooper.

BOONE COUNTY

Organized: 1830
Named for: Daniel Boone
Major cities and towns: Lebanon, Zionsville, Thorntown

■ Eight vast pillars allude to the towering lime-stone columns of the Boone County Courthouse in Lebanon, designed by architect Joseph T. Hutton. Upon completion in 1911, the courthouse's 38-foot pillars—then thought to be the largest one-piece limestone columns in the world—attracted specta-tors from around the globe. In this piece, a band encircling several of the columns acknowledges the Second Principal Meridian, a survey line used to create township boundaries after the U.S. Congress' Land Ordinance of 1785. The meridian extends north and south from a point south of Paoli in Orange County, and passes directly through Boone County's Courthouse.

Jemerson

All eight of the Boone County Courthouse's columns were cut from a single piece of Indiana limestone measuring 80 feet in length.

ARTIST'S NOTES

The sandstone used in this sculpture was obtained from a recently reopened Parke County quarry in Mansfield, Indiana.

BROWN COUNTY

Organized: 1836
Named for: Jacob Jennings Brown
Major cities and towns: Nashville

■ Delicate limestone leaves in this piece's background represent Brown County's many acres of beautifully colored, scenic woodlands. A brown sandstone paint palette pays tribute to the artists and craftspeople who have flocked to these picturesque hills for inspiration since the 1870s. Forming the nucleus of an art colony that continues today, T.C. Steele and Adolph Shulz moved their families here in 1907. Steele's home, "The House of the Singing Winds," and surrounding property is today a state historic site. The palette in this artwork also doubles as a mandolin body, recognizing the contributions made to Brown County by legendary musician Bill Monroe, who organized the first Bean Blossom Bluegrass Festival here in 1967.

LARAMORE

 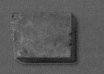

MATERIALS USED:
Sandstone, Limestone, Silicon Bronze

CARROLL COUNTY

Organized: 1828
Named for: Charles Carroll
Major cities and towns: Delphi, Flora, Camden

■ Against a ridged, patchwork background—emblematic of the county's formidable farming heritage—bronze soybean pods rest alongside a sparkling, tiled lake. The structure's blue ceramic chips echo the rippling waters of Lake Freeman, a 2,800-acre man-made reservoir located in Carroll and neighboring White County. Small white triangles in the piece represent the boats of contented sailors.

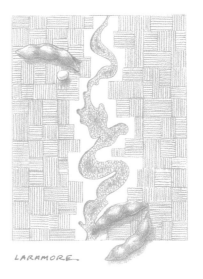

LARAMORE

The porcelain tile in the Carroll County piece was painstakingly glued into the artwork after being broken up with hammers.

ARTIST'S NOTES

The Cass County piece was originally intended to include small bronze railroad tracks, but the artist changed his mind after viewing the carved limestone's eloquent simplicity.

CASS COUNTY

Organized: 1829
Named for: Lewis Cass
Major cities and towns: Logansport, Galveston, Walton

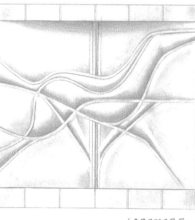

LARAMORE

■ Criss-crossing paths in this all-limestone piece form a distinctly horse-like shape, making reference to a colorful carousel that arrived in Cass County circa 1919. The ride's 42 wooden animals, created by German artisan Gustav Dentzel, have been recently refurbished, and still whirl today in Logansport's Riverside Park.

■ The intersections of various lines suggest the area's early influence as a significant Midwestern transportation center. The winding Wabash River was used as a trade route, and the major north-south Michigan Road reached here in 1832. By 1838, the Wabash and Erie Canal had come to county seat Logansport, and Cass County's first railroads were built in the 1850s. For many years, the region hosted such lines as the Pennsylvania, the Wabash, the Vandalia and the Cincinnati, Logansport and Chicago.

Cass County's Gustav Dentzel-designed carousel arrived in Logansport's Spencer Park around 1919. In 1950, the carousel was moved to its present home in Riverside Park. Open seasonally, the ride was added to the National Register of Historic Places in 1987.

ARTIST'S NOTES

Located in a steeply inclined fountain west of the museum's main entrance, this piece was masterfully assembled from layered, laser-cut metal frameworks by Indianapolis mechanical designer Rob Miller.

CLARK COUNTY

Organized: 1801
Named for: George Rogers Clark
Major cities and towns: Jeffersonville, Clarksville, Sellersburg, Charlestown

■ Ascending a steep waterfall, a paddlewheel steamboat makes its way, fish-like, upstream. This Clark County piece salutes the city of Jeffersonville, North America's largest inland boat-building site. The lines of the ascending steamboat, designed to simulate a raised topographic map, reflect the hilly landscape of southern Indiana. The fountain itself calls to mind the Falls of the Ohio, a stretch of the Ohio River that drops 22 feet over two miles.

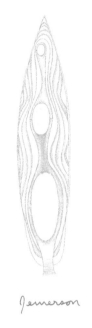

Jemerson

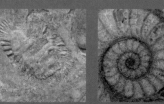

A fossilized coral reef more than 350 million years old lies exposed along the river's banks, in Falls of the Ohio State Park.

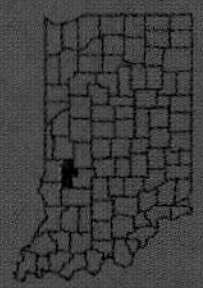

ARTIST'S NOTES

The arrangement of elements in this sculpture suggests a stylized human face.

CLAY COUNTY

Organized: 1825
Named for: Henry Clay
Major cities and towns: Brazil, Clay City, Knightsville

■ Protruding slightly, a slanted square of bricks is bisected by ceramic piping and painted pottery. A fine grade of clay, discovered in Clay County during the 19th century, provided raw material for a number of pottery and brick factories. A single lump of black coal near the piece's right edge pays homage to the area's rich coal deposits, which have made mining an important industry here since the 1850s.

LARAMORE.

The business of Clay City Pottery, Incorporated was begun by Beryl Griffith in 1885. For four generations, the Griffith family has continued to manufacture its pottery from local clay.

Clinton County

Organized in 1830
Named for DeWitt Clinton

"Old Stoney" was opened in 1912 as a junior and senior high school.
The building represents a rare combination of several architectural styles,
simulating a limestone, castle-like appearance. Six years after closing,
"Old Stoney" reopened in 1993 as the home of the Clinton County
Historical Society and Museum.

CLINTON COUNTY

Organized: 1830
Named for: De Witt Clinton
Major cities and towns: Frankfort, Rossville, Mulberry

■ Against a scored limestone background, a red frankfurter is toasted on the tower of an imposing building. Clinton County's sculpture tells the story of "Old Stoney," a castle-like Frankfort landmark that opened in 1892 as a junior and senior high school (home of the Frankfort Hot Dogs). Gutted by fire in 1922, the structure's interior was renovated, and continued in use as a school until 1974. Today, the building houses the Clinton County Historical Society and Museum.

Jemerson

Old Stoney was the alma mater of actor and political activist Will Geer, born in Frankfort in 1902, and best known for playing the grandfather on the 1970s television series The Waltons.

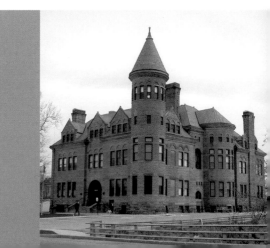

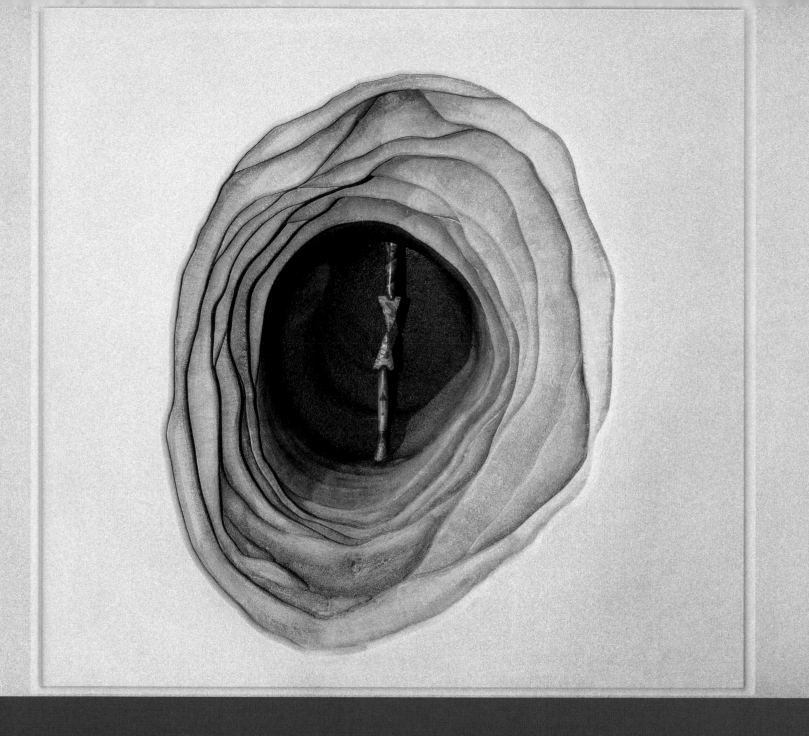

ARTIST'S NOTES

Due to its subterranean subject matter, Crawford County's piece utilizes negative space, rather than a raised three-dimensional form.

CRAWFORD COUNTY

Organized: 1818
Named for: William Crawford
Major cities and towns: Marengo, English, Milltown, Leavenworth

■ Two arrowheads meet and merge over a hole in the stone, paying tribute to Crawford County's Marengo and Wyandotte Caves. Prehistoric Native Americans mined Wyandotte Cave for flint, using the mineral to create weapons, tools and other artifacts. The same cavern also is home to 135-foot-tall Monument Mountain, the largest underground mountain on earth.

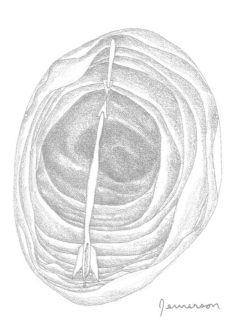

13

MATERIALS USED:
Wood, Copper, Limestone

ARTIST'S NOTES

A slightly asymmetrical placement of tiles has lent the Daviess County sculpture a human element.

DAVIESS COUNTY

Organized: 1817
Named for: Joseph Hamilton Daviess
Major cities and towns: Washington, Odon, Elnora

■ A mosaic of colorful ceramic tiles creates the pattern of a large, fan-tailed turkey, acknowledging the agricultural heritage of Daviess County. Home to one of the Midwest's largest turkey farms, the area hosts a Turkey Trot festival each fall in the town of Montgomery. The turkey's tail also simulates a quilt pattern, paying tribute to the county's sizeable Amish population.

Jemerson

JOSEPH HAMILTON DAVIESS

A lawyer by trade, Joseph Hamilton Daviess served as Kentucky's district attorney before volunteering for the Kentucky militia. As a major, he led several troops north to a site near present-day Lafayette, Indiana. He died there, in the Battle of Tippecanoe, in 1811.

ARTIST'S NOTES

A skilled machinist helped to fabricate this piece's piston-like figures.

DEARBORN COUNTY

Organized: 1803
Named for: Henry Dearborn
Major cities and towns: Lawrenceburg, Greendale, Aurora, Dillsboro

■ Steam-piston-like structures line the periphery of the Dearborn County piece, a tribute to the ornate steamboats that once traveled the nearby Ohio River. In the mid-1850s, industrialist Thomas Gaff—who used a fleet of these "floating palaces" to transport his goods—commissioned the building of Hillforest Mansion, a magnificent two-story home in Aurora, Indiana. Appropriately, the porch of his two-story home bears a more-than-passing resemblance to the deck of a steamboat.

ARTIST'S NOTES

The bronze tree at the tip of Decatur County's piece has been treated with a patina, causing it to turn green.

DECATUR COUNTY

Organized: 1821
Named for: Stephen Decatur
Major cities and towns: Greensburg, Westport

■ High above the earth, an elongated spire—which, in turn, sprouts a small bronze tree from its tip—seems to grow organically out of the museum's wall. This piece commemorates the series of large-tooth aspen trees that have grown atop the Decatur County Courthouse's 115-foot-clock tower since 1870. Each September, the county seat of Greensburg celebrates its civic vegetation with the Tree City Fall Festival.

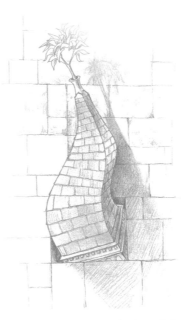

LARAMORE

The Decatur County Courthouse was designed by Indianapolis architect Edwin May between 1854 and 1860, at a cost of $120,000. May later laid out the Indiana State House.

The "flying lady" in the DeKalb County piece was patterned after a hood ornament used by the Auburn Automobile Company.

DeKalb County

Organized in 1837

Named for Baron Johann de Kalb

Although 80 percent of the county's land is used for farming, the city of Auburn was once a major center of the American automobile industry. More than 21 models of cars were crafted here, including the elegant Auburn and the classic Cord.

DEKALB COUNTY

Organized: 1837
Named for: Baron Johann de Kalb
Major cities and towns: Auburn, Garrett, Butler, Waterloo

■ High above a furrowed bed of freshly plowed farm-land, a streamlined, bronze hood ornament glides nobly. Although much of DeKalb County's land is used for farming, the city of Auburn was, from 1900 to 1937, a major center of America's automobile industry. This piece salutes the Auburn, Cord and other cars that were once manufactured here.

Since 1974, DeKalb County's Auburn Cord Duesenberg museum has showcased over 100 classic cars in the former headquarters of the Auburn Automobile Company.

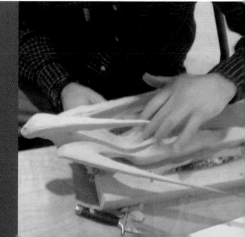

ARTIST'S NOTES

Pickles were chosen as the jarred vegetables of Delaware County's piece, due to the contrast of their green color with the bright orange Garfield.

DELAWARE COUNTY

Organized: 1827
Named for: The Delaware Tribe
Major cities and towns: Muncie, Yorktown, Albany

■ Following a series of eight pickle-filled jars, a ninth container holds a baffled image of the famously gluttonous Garfield the Cat. A light-hearted tribute to Delaware County, this piece commemorates the home canning and glass jar industries that moved here following the discovery of natural gas in the late 1880s. Garfield is the creation of Hoosier cartoonist Jim Davis, who attended college in county seat Muncie, and currently operates his company, Paws, Inc., in Albany, Indiana.

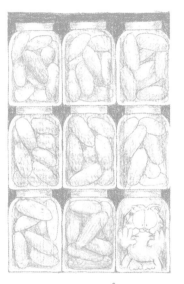

THE DELAWARE TRIBE

The Lenape, a group of Native Americans, once lived in the area of the Delaware River and Delaware Bay, in what is now the eastern United States. Pushed west by settlers, this group of people, referred to by whites as the Delaware, settled in what is now eastern Ohio, and established villages to the west in what became Indiana (including the Delaware County settlement of Munsee Town).

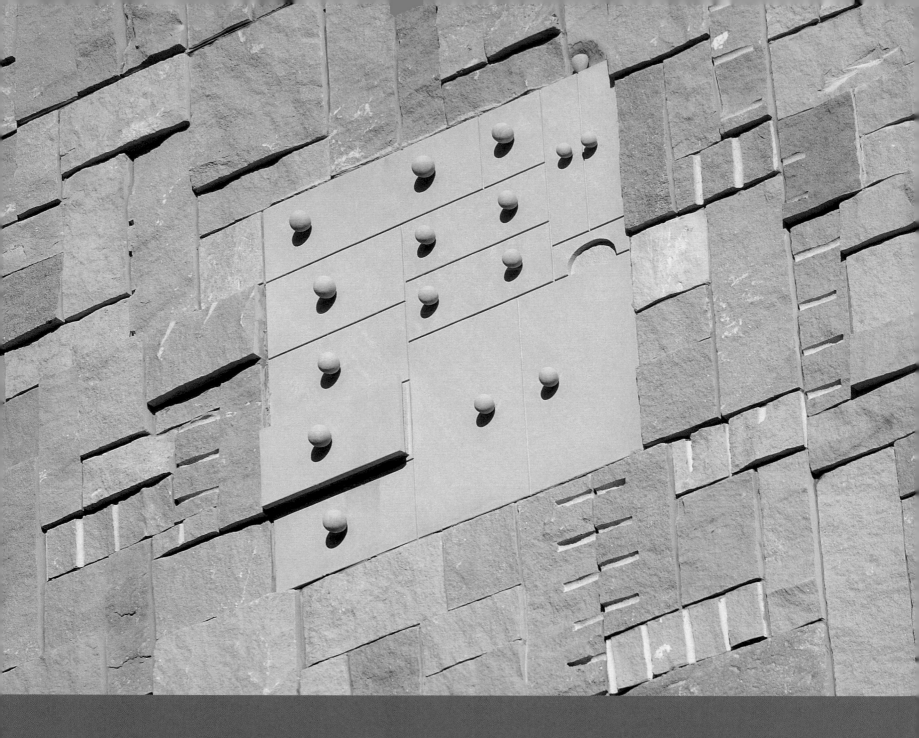

ARTIST'S NOTES

Though texturally different, the shapes and sizes of the drawers in the Dubois County piece are similar to those of the pieces of limestone in the wall surrounding them.

DUBOIS COUNTY

Organized: 1818
Named for: Toussaint Dubois
Major cities and towns: Jasper, Huntingburg, Ferdinand

■ With one drawer slightly ajar, this smooth limestone cabinet stands in sharp contrast to the rough limestone surrounding it. Dubois County is home to large manufacturers of pianos, organs and furniture, and this piece reflects the area's woodworking tradition. Since the region also is one of the state's largest poultry-producing counties, the drawer pulls are designed to resemble carved limestone eggs.

Jemerson

19

Kimball International, one of Dubois County's most noted furniture manufacturers, designed many of the furnishings used within the Indiana State Museum.

ARTIST'S NOTES

The artist briefly considered incorporating Alka-Seltzer into this piece's design, in deference to the pain reliever's original maker. Miles Laboratories was established in Elkhart County in 1884 by Dr. Franklin Miles.

ELKHART COUNTY

Organized: 1830
Named for: The Elkhart River
Major cities and towns: Elkhart, Goshen, Nappanee, Middlebury

■ Here, a twisting bronze horn twines sinuously, wrapping itself into the musical symbol of a treble clef. Elkhart County, a center of musical instrument manufacturing, has long been known as the "band instrument capital of the world." The area also is a hub of recreational vehicle fabrication, and the small wheels and windows at the base of this piece acknowledge the more than 200 firms in the area that manufacture mobile homes, campers and other RV-related products.

LARAMORE

Elkhart has been the manufacturing center for many familiar brands of musical instruments, including Conn, Selmer and Ludwig.

ARTIST'S NOTES

The bronze handle on the car door simulates a cabinet knob.

FAYETTE COUNTY

Organized: 1819
Named for: Marquis de Lafayette
Major cities and towns: Connersville

In Fayette County's piece, an antique car's ornately carved door stands slightly ajar. Due to the forests that originally stood here, the region attracted many furniture manufacturers in the early 1900s. In addition, the county seat of Connersville was once home to many different automobile manufacturers—among them such makes as Lexington and McFarlan.

LARAMORE

MARQUIS DE LAFAYETTE

Marie Joseph Paul Yves Roch Gilbert du Motier, Marquis de Lafayette, left France for America in 1777, determined to assist the colonists' revolution. He served at Valley Forge and the battles of Brandywine and Yorktown, becoming friends with George Washington in the process. After the American Revolution was won, Lafayette returned to France, where he played an important role in the French Revolution as well. From July 1824 to September 1825, Lafayette toured the U.S., visiting Jeffersonville, Indiana in May 1825.

ARTIST'S NOTES

The blue-green color of the glass mimics the knobs' appearance in springtime and summer.

FLOYD COUNTY

Organized: 1819
Named for: Davis Floyd
Major cities and towns: New Albany, Georgetown

■ A collection of steep blue hills rising from the wall's surface conjures images of a colorful topographic map. Knobs, large land formations created by glacier melt water, are a distinctive geographic feature in southeastern Indiana—and the town of Floyds Knobs, in Indiana's Floyd County, is well-known for them. In the late 1860s, the county seat of New Albany became home to American Plate Glass Works, the nation's first plate glass factory.

Jemerson

Some of Floyd County's larger formations include Lost Knob, Spickert Knob and Bald Knob.

ARTIST'S NOTES

Using great delicacy, Bloomington metal sculptor Alex Black fabricated this piece's handsome bronze framework, into which stained glass was carefully placed. The Fountain County artwork is one of few pieces that may be viewed from the outside or (should you happen to be visiting the gift shop) the inside of the museum.

FOUNTAIN COUNTY

Organized: 1825
Named for: Major James Fountain
Major cities and towns: Attica, Covington, Veedersburg

■ The curved bronze arc of this piece recalls the Portland Arch, a massive sandstone formation that is one of the state's few National Natural Landmarks. Created over millions of years by a small stream, this natural bridge is located on the south side of the town of Fountain, in the Portland Arch Nature Preserve. Fountain County also boasts a lengthy agricultural heritage, which is honored here by colorful, stylized ears of corn.

ARTIST'S NOTES

The Franklin County piece is suspended from a bridge that crosses downtown Indianapolis'
Central Canal——making it a canal over a creek, under a bridge over a canal.

FRANKLIN COUNTY

Organized: 1811
Named for: Benjamin Franklin
Major cities and towns: Brookville, Batesville, Oldenburg, Laurel

■ Floating in the air, a copper canal boat sails serenely over a covered bridge. In 1848, Whitewater Canal stockholders built an 80-foot-long aqueduct to carry the canal above Duck Creek. One of several canal projects initiated by Indiana's Mammoth Internal Improvements Act of 1836, the Whitewater Canal eventually stretched some 76 miles between Lawrenceburg and Hagerstown. Visitors to the Franklin County town of Metamora may still view a portion of this canal, now a state historic site.

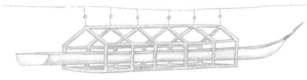

Jemerson

MATERIALS USED:
Copper, Bronze, Stainless Steel

ARTIST'S NOTES

Mimicking the appearance of an aged barn, gaps between slats in this piece's sides allow light and air to pass through. The delicate curvature of Fulton County's artwork was fabricated by metal sculptor David Bellamy of Knightstown.

FULTON COUNTY

Organized: 1836
Named for: Robert Fulton
Major cities and towns: Rochester, Akron, Kewanna

■ Sunlight glints off the roof of a round bronze barn, honoring some of Fulton County's more distinctive landmarks. Many of the round barns that dotted this region at the turn of the 20th century still remain. At the barn's peak, a sailboat serves as a weather vane, paying tribute to the water sports and other recreations enjoyed on Lake Manitou, near the town of Kewanna.

LARAMORE

Even before the arrival of white settlers, there were rumors of gigantic water creatures living in the depths of Lake Manitou. Monster sightings fell off sharply following the capture of two enormous fish in 1849 and 1888.

Houses, a church and a gushing oil well are all visible in this piece.

GIBSON COUNTY

Organized: 1813
Named for: John Gibson
Major cities and towns: Princeton, Oakland City, Fort Branch, Haubstadt, Owensville

■ Jostling one another for space, a collection of closely set structures creates the effect of a stylized tribal mask. From the mid-1800s until the early 1950s, the bustling African-American community of Lyles Station thrived in Gibson County. The region also is home to large coal and oil reserves, and pump jacks became a common sight near the city of Princeton after oil was struck there in 1903.

Lyles Station was founded by Joshua and Sanford Lyles, former slaves from Tennessee. The church played an important role in sustaining the community, which boasted a population of approximately 800 persons at its peak.

ARTIST'S NOTES

The Grant County artwork was the first limestone piece to be sculpted.

GRANT COUNTY

Organized: 1831
Named for: Samuel and Moses Grant
Major cities and towns: Marion, Gas City, Upland, Fairmount

▪ Exploding out of their container, bursting kernels of movie popcorn form the iconic profile of native son James Dean. Dean, born in the Grant County town of Marion in 1931, grew up in the

nearby town of Fairmount before leaving for Hollywood, where he starred in such watershed 1950s films as *Rebel Without a Cause, East of Eden* and *Giant*. A festival in Dean's honor is held annually in the county (which also is home to one of the world's largest popcorn producers).

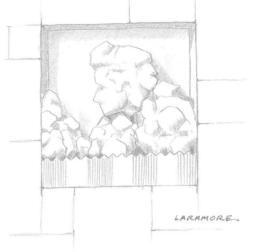

James Dean's grave site, located in Fairmount's Park Cemetery, is visited by thousands of fans each year.

GREENE COUNTY

Organized: 1821
Named for: Nathaniel Greene
Major cities and towns: Linton, Bloomfield, Jasonville, Worthington

■ Supported by a thick, leafy brace, a series of train cars glide along the top of a vast, delicately carved span. In 1906, the Illinois Central Railroad constructed one of the world's largest railroad bridges near Solsberry, in Greene County. Until 1924, the county also was home to the nation's largest deciduous tree, a gigantic sycamore in the town of Worthington.

LARAMORE

A branch of the nation's largest deciduous tree is still preserved in Worthington's City Park, in a shelter at the intersection of Dayton and Worthington Streets.

ARTIST'S NOTES

The Hamilton County sculpture is composed of different-colored pieces of sandstone — which, like limestone, is indigenous to Indiana.

HAMILTON COUNTY

Organized: 1823
Named for: Alexander Hamilton
Major cities and towns: Fishers, Carmel, Noblesville, Westfield

■ Balanced atop a small cabin, a puzzle-like, towering cluster of suburban homes spreads out in all directions. When trader William Conner arrived here around 1801, the surrounding land was prairie and wilderness. Though farming still dominates large portions of Hamilton County, the later years of the 20th century saw much of the area develop into residential suburbs of Indianapolis.

The Conner Prairie Living History Museum stands in the town of Fishers, on land once owned by settler William Conner. Since 1974, the recreated village of Prairietown has offered visitors a glimpse of life in 19th century Indiana.

ARTIST'S NOTES

Small pieces of turquoise stone simulate the poet's blue eyes.

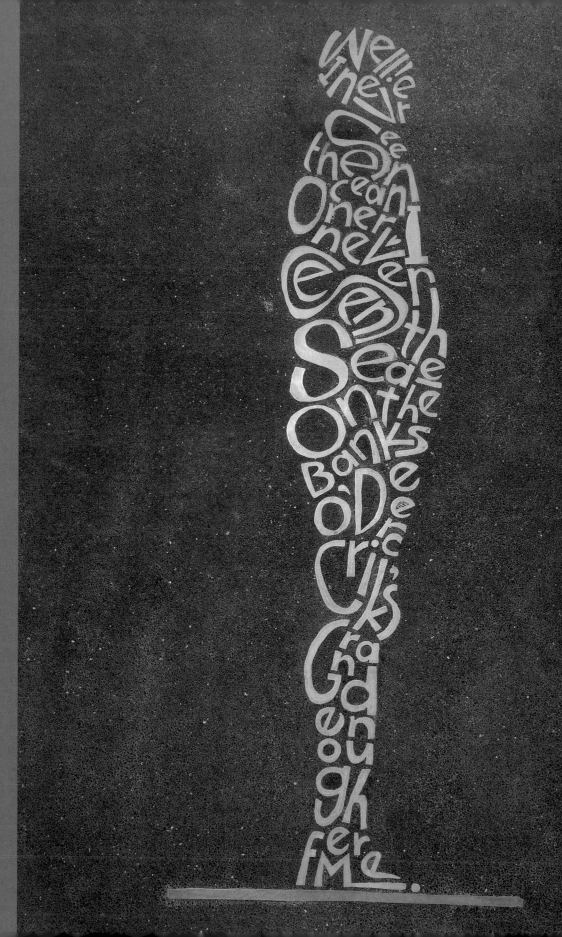

HANCOCK COUNTY

Organized: 1828
Named for: John Hancock
Major cities and towns: Greenfield, Fortville, Cumberland, New Palestine

■ Flowing out one after another, the words of a poetic refrain take on human shape, eventually forming a man's silhouette. James Whitcomb Riley, the "Hoosier Poet," was born in the Hancock County town of Greenfield in 1849. "Little Orphant Annie," "The Old Swimmin' Hole," and Riley's other poems about rural Indiana life—many of them written in dialect—were wildly popular in the late 19th century, and Riley became a top draw on the national lecture circuit.

Jemerson

The words used in this piece form the refrain of Riley's composition, "On The Banks O' Deer Crick," a poem that reflects the author's appreciation for the subtle pleasures of the Midwestern landscape.

Well!—I never seen the ocean ner I never seen the Sea.—
On the banks o' Deer Crick's grand enough fer me!

HARRISON COUNTY

Organized: 1808
Named for: William Henry Harrison
Major cities and towns: Corydon, Palmyra, Lanesville, Milltown

■ In this piece, two crossed sabres clash above a bold capital star—a reference to the only Civil War battle fought in Indiana. On July 9, 1863, Confederate raiders led by Brig. Gen. John Hunt Morgan met and overwhelmed about 400 members of the Harrison County Home Guard before marching into the county seat of Corydon.

■ It also was in Corydon, 39 years earlier, that Indiana's first constitutional convention was held. Following approval of a new constitution on June 29, 1816, Indiana became our nation's 19th state. Corydon, which had served as capital of the Indiana Territory since May 1813, then acted as the state's first capital until 1825.

LARAMORE.

The city of Corydon's state historic site includes a capitol building erected between 1814 and 1816. The structure hosted the drafting of Indiana's first state constitution in June 1816, and housed the first General Assembly later that year. Corydon's state historic site also includes a structure built in 1817, later occupied by Indiana's second elected governor, William Hendricks, as his living quarters and office.

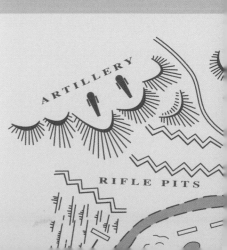

ARTIST'S NOTES

When fabricating this piece, Todd Ketchum of Santarossa Mosaic and Tile made use of the material rustic terrazzo—a cousin to concrete. By expertly mixing colors, Ketchum was able to realize the artist's original creative vision.

HENDRICKS COUNTY

Organized: 1824
Named for: William Hendricks
Major cities and towns: Plainfield, Brownsburg, Danville, Avon

■ From town to town, from day until night, a well-traveled strip of numbered black highway stretches across the countryside. Route 40—the old National Road—runs through the southern section of Hendricks County, eventually passing by the south lawn of the state museum itself. Set, appropriately, in the sidewalk, this piece is oriented parallel to the very road it represents.

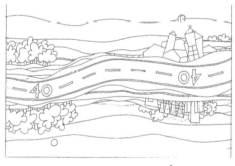

Jemerson

WILLIAM HENDRICKS

Born in Pennsylvania, William Hendricks came to Madison, Indiana as a young man, and served as one of Indiana's members in the U.S. House of Representatives from 1816 until 1822. He later served as Indiana's governor (1822–1825) and as a United States senator from Indiana (1825–1837). Besides helping to create Hanover College and Indiana University at Bloomington, Hendricks worked hard to build Indiana roads and canals.

ARTIST'S NOTES

Subtle wheels along the sides of this piece honor Henry County's automotive heritage. A 1907 auto plant in New Castle, which originally manufactured Maxwell automobiles, has produced Chrysler products since 1925.

HENRY COUNTY

Organized: 1822
Named for: Patrick Henry
Major cities and towns: New Castle, Middletown, Knightstown

■ Atop the playing floor of a worn high school basketball court, the Wright Brothers' first powered airplane rolls to a stop. Along with his younger brother Orville, Wilbur Wright—born in 1867 near the Henry County town of Millville—created aviation history with his 1903 flight. This straightforward piece also honors county seat New Castle, home to the Indiana High School Basketball Hall of Fame.

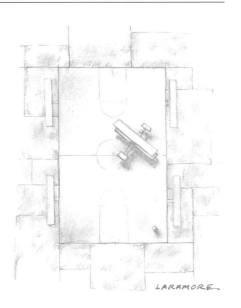

LARAMORE

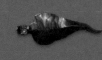 

MATERIALS USED:
Bronze, Limestone, Copper

The contours of Howard County's piece also contain an abstract, questioning face.

HOWARD COUNTY

Organized: 1844
Named for: Tilghman A. Howard
Major cities and towns: Kokomo, Greentown, Russiaville

■ Within the shape of a limestone light bulb, a winding bronze filament forms the shape of a primitive automobile and driver. Kokomo, the county seat of Howard County, is known as the "City of Firsts," and one of inventor Elwood Haynes' more famous inspirational flashes resulted in Indiana's first commercially built, gasoline-powered automobile. In 1894, the car reached speeds of six to seven miles per hour on a six-mile stretch of Pumpkinville Pike, leading southeast from Kokomo. Here, Haynes and his vehicle are immortalized together in a tribute to Hoosier ingenuity.

LARAMORE

Elwood Haynes also invented stainless steel (1911) and Stellite (1906), a high-performance nickel-chromium alloy. Other famous Kokomo firsts include the creation of the pneumatic rubber tire (D.C. Spraker, 1894), the carburetor (George Kingston, 1902), the howitzer shell (Superior Machine Tool Co., 1918), the mechanical corn picker (John Powell, 1920), Dirilyte Golden-Hued Tableware (Carl Molin, 1926) and canned tomato juice (Walter Kemp, 1928).

HUNTINGTON COUNTY

Organized: 1834
Named for: Samuel Huntington
Major cities and towns: Huntington, Roanoke, Andrews, Warren

■ Three Native Americans pilot canoes around this shield-like piece, circumnavigating the fork of three currents. The presence of the Wabash and Salamonie Rivers made this area a popular trading center for Native Americans, and in 1831, Chief John Baptiste Richardville moved the Miami's capital to a site at the Forks of the Wabash, in what later became Huntington County. White settlers arrived here in the middle of the 19th century, bringing with them the Wabash & Erie Canal.

LARAMORE

For millennia, the Forks of the Wabash served as a camping ground for Native Americans. By 1700, the Miami had laid claim to the entire Wabash Valley and later traded with French explorers who arrived in the area.

ARTIST'S NOTES

The dimensional relief in this limestone piece features four elevations of carving.

JACKSON COUNTY

Organized: 1816
Named for: Andrew Jackson
Major cities and towns: Seymour, Brownstown, Crothersville

■ Five human figures peer stealthily around trees, as spoked wheels appear behind a dense growth of foliage. This multi-leveled piece pays tribute to an event that occurred near Seymour on October 6, 1866, when the tranquil, wooded hills of Jackson County witnessed the nation's first train robbery, conducted by the locally-based Reno Gang.

The Jackson-Washington State Forest, which covers nearly 17,000 acres in Jackson and neighboring Washington County, includes a large portion of the 58-mile Knobstone Trail—Indiana's longest footpath.

*A patina applied to the bronze
has caused this piece to green, and
contributed to a natural feel.*

JASPER COUNTY

Organized: 1838
Named for: William Jasper
Major cities and towns: Rensselaer, De Motte, Remington

■ Camouflaged against tall reeds, two long-legged birds stand erect—somewhat reminiscent of treble clef signs on a musical staff. Each fall, tens of thousands of sandhill cranes pause in their migration south to visit the shallow marshes of Jasper County's Jasper-Pulaski Fish and Wildlife Area. The region also was home to Rensselaer-born composer James F. Hanley, who—inspired by Paul Dresser's 1898 hit, "On the Banks of the Wabash"—joined with lyricist Ballard MacDonald to pen "(Back Home Again in) Indiana" in 1917.

LARAMORE

ARTIST'S NOTES

Different colors and textures of glass were used to create this piece. The stained glass is not leaded, but copper-foiled.

JAY COUNTY

Organized: 1836
Named for: John Jay
Major cities and towns: Portland, Dunkirk, Redkey

■ Colorful, many-textured flames leap upward in this circular stained glass piece. Home of Indiana's first drilled natural gas well, Jay County effectively launched the state's gas boom in 1886. The town of Dunkirk became known as the "glass capital of Indiana," and the county courthouse in Portland features a magnificent stained glass rotunda dome, constructed between 1915 and 1919 by architects McLaughlin and Hulsken.

Jemerson

38

In 1886, Indiana's first gas well was drilled in the town of Portland, near the intersection of present-day Depot and North streets. The well launched a lucrative Indiana gas boom, which brought many businesses to the state until resources became depleted in the early 1900s.

ARTIST'S NOTES

This piece's vertical format reflects the steep grade of the Madison railroad incline, coupled with the sheer plunge of Clifty Creek's waterfalls.

JEFFERSON COUNTY

Organized: 1811
Named for: Thomas Jefferson
Major cities and towns: Madison, Hanover

■ Against a backdrop of cascading water, one determined loco-motive draws its coal car upwards, from the river below to the bluffs above. In 1836, work began on one of Indiana's first rail-roads, the Madison and Indianapolis. To haul cars up from the Ohio River Valley, workers cut into Jefferson County's high bluffs, laying track on a 1.3 mile incline that rose 311 feet per mile, and constructing one of the United States' steepest-ever standard gauge railroads. The region also is home to Clifty Falls State Park, a 1,361-acre area that includes a deep, bouldered ravine and four of the state's major waterfalls.

LARAMORE.

39

In 1866, the Madison and Indianapolis Railroad merged with the Jeffersonville Railroad, forming the Jeffersonville, Madison and Indianapolis. The Reuben Wells, an 1868 locomotive designed by and named after the line's master mechanic, was used regularly on the Madison incline until 1905.

ARTIST'S NOTES

Man's presence has made a
sanctuary out of the Muscatatuck
area's wilderness—hence, the artist's
inclusion of subtle human figures
in the background of this piece.

JENNINGS COUNTY

Organized: 1817
Named for: Jonathan Jennings
Major cities and towns: North Vernon, Vernon

■ Bursting from the water, two fish hurl their bodies skyward, blending their forms into the wings and body of a long-limbed water bird. In 1966, Jennings County became home for much of the Muscatatuck National Wildlife Refuge. Today, the nearly 7,800-acre sanctuary serves as a haven for fish, native and migratory birds and other wildlife.

40

JONATHAN JENNINGS

As a young man, Jonathan Jennings studied law in Jeffersonville, Indiana. In 1807, he began a law practice in Vincennes, and soon moved to Clark County. For three terms, he served as a territorial delegate to Congress. When Indiana became a state in 1816, Jennings was elected as its first governor. He resigned from that office in 1822 to serve as Indiana's representative to Congress.

ARTIST'S NOTES

The shells of the three turtles (cast from actual military helmets) were placed on a low wall of the museum, so that the whimsical sculptures would be easily visible to children.

JOHNSON COUNTY

Organized: 1822
Named for: John Johnson
Major cities and towns: Greenwood, Franklin, New Whiteland, Edinburgh

■ The helmet-like shells of three marching turtles honor Johnson County's Camp Atterbury, a military training ground that has been partially reclaimed as a nature preserve. Opened in 1942, the 40,351-acre installation helped prepare some 275,000 soldiers for U.S. Army service in World War II. Much of the area is still used as a training facility for the National Guard and Army Reserve, but 6,206 acres of land purchased by the state of Indiana in 1969 now serve as the Atterbury Fish and Wildlife Area, providing a natural habitat for fish, birds and many other animals.

41

During World War II, Camp Atterbury also served as an internment camp for thousands of Italian and German prisoners of war. In 1943, Italian prisoners constructed a small house of worship here, dubbed the "Chapel in the Meadow."

The neckpiece of the Native American in Knox County's piece doubles as a compass, the needle of which faces northwest.

KNOX COUNTY

Organized: 1790
Named for: Henry Knox
Major cities and towns: Vincennes, Bicknell

42

■ The borders and contours of a raised territory map form the features of a Native American man, reflecting the historic role the Knox County region has played in American history. It was in this area, originally populated by Native Americans, that the city of Vincennes was established in 1732 by Frenchmen seeking to build a trading post equidistant from New Orleans, Detroit and St. Louis. Vincennes, the county seat, remains the oldest permanent European settlement in what is now Indiana.

LARAMORE.

■ The French and Indian War—an alliance of French and Native Americans fighting the British from 1754 to 1763—ended with the Treaty of Paris, which awarded England control of Canada and all land east of the Mississippi River (including present-day Indiana). However, American George Rogers Clark's 1779 defeat of British forces at Vincennes' Fort Sackville secured control of the region for the United States. The Ordinance of 1787 established the Northwest Territory, an area that included all lands northwest of the Ohio River. In 1800, Vincennes became the first capital of the new Indiana Territory.

The many components of the Vincennes State Historic Sites include the Indiana Territory Capitol (centered around the "Red House," a preserved meeting place of the 1811 legislature), the Print Shop of Elihu Stout (a Vincennes printer who began publishing his Indiana Gazette *newspaper in 1804) and the relocated birthplace of Maurice Thompson (author of the popular 1900 novel,* Alice of Old Vincennes*).*

ARTIST'S NOTES

The artist studied maps of Kosciusko County's lakes before sculpting the limestone globe's watery portions.

KOSCIUSKO COUNTY

Organized: 1836
Named for: Thaddeus Kosciuszko
Major cities and towns: Warsaw, Winona Lake, Syracuse, Milford

■ Straining dutifully, a sturdy bronze farmer holds a water-covered, egg-shaped globe aloft on his strapping shoulders. Metaphorically, eggs mean the world to Kosciusko County, a largely farming region that prides itself on its substantial hatch egg, poultry meat and egg processing businesses. The county also is home to more than 100 lakes—including Indiana's largest natural lake, Lake Wawasee, and its deepest, Lake Tippecanoe.

LARAMORE.

43

The Kosciusko County town of Mentone is home to a 3,000-pound, 12-foot-tall concrete egg. Created in 1946 to promote Mentone's annual Egg Festival, the sculpture is inscribed with the words, "Egg Basket of the Midwest."

ARTIST'S NOTES

The fierce animals at the corners of the LaGrange County piece were an effort to provide the State Museum with its own protective gargoyles.

LaGrange County

Organized in 1832
Named for LaGrange-Barenn

A multitude of farms in LaGrange County are owned by members of the Mennonite and Amish church communities. First arriving from Pennsylvania in 1841, the Amish and Mennonites have continuously farmed these dairy and livestock farms. The Amish-based Shipshewana Auction has become a tourist attraction, featuring antiques and collectibles.

LAGRANGE COUNTY

Organized: 1832
Named for: LaGrange-Bleneau
Major cities and towns: LaGrange, Topeka, Shipshewana

■ Amid soybeans and corn kernels, the heads of four imposing farm animals stand guard over a crate of colorful bric-a-brac. The flea markets and auctions held in the town of Shipshewana attract thousands of visitors each year to LaGrange County, a region that also is noted for its long-standing farming traditions. The quilt-like appearance of the piece pays homage to the area's sizeable Amish population, well known for its production of handcrafted bedcovers and other crafts.

Jemerson

Objects used to create this artwork include a corncob pipe, a Wendell Willkie campaign button, a still-ticking watch and a small pair of ruby slippers liberated from the desk of State Budget Director Betty Cockrum, who was born and reared in LaGrange County.

ARTIST'S NOTES

Before designing this piece, the artist spent considerable time studying the motion of waves.

LAKE COUNTY

Organized: 1836
Named for: Lake Michigan
Major cities and towns: Gary, Hammond, East Chicago, Merrillville, Hobart

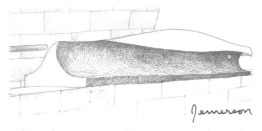

■ Like the head of a body-surfer, one stainless steel sphere bobs beneath the delicate curl of a limestone wave. Lake County borders the southern tip of Lake Michigan, providing ports for the export and import of goods. Due to the mills and foundries that came to this county in the early 20th century, Indiana has ranked among the nation's top steel-producing states.

ARTIST'S NOTES

The LaPorte County piece contains an actual 360° rotating light.

LAPORTE COUNTY

Organized: 1832
Named for: An area where thick forests opened into open prairie. Early French explorers called this region "la porte," or "the door."
Major cities and towns: Michigan City, LaPorte, Trail Creek, Westville

■ Through all weather, in all hours of day and night, the beam from a vigilant beacon shines out high atop the museum's northwest wall. In 1858, the United States government built a stone and brick lighthouse in the LaPorte County town of Michigan City (replacing an earlier edifice erected in 1837), and this piece salutes that structure—which still stands on the shore of Lake Michigan.

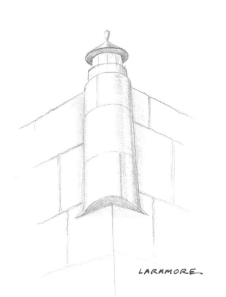

LARAMORE

When the Indiana Territory achieved statehood in 1816, Congress moved the state's boundary ten miles north, giving Indiana part of Lake Michigan.

The Empire State Building's tower also may be interpreted as the capsule's vapor trail.

LAWRENCE COUNTY

Organized: 1818
Named for: James Lawrence
Major cities and towns: Bedford, Mitchell, Oolitic

■ Here, a distinctive spire reminiscent of the Empire State Building is capped by a soaring spacecraft, straining toward a distant orb. Lawrence County's limestone quarries have provided building materials for some of the world's most famous structures. In addition, the county has produced several astronauts, including Kenneth Bowersox, Charles Walker and Virgil "Gus" Grissom, one of the original Mercury astronauts chosen by NASA in 1959.

LARAMORE.

47

The first commercial limestone quarrying in Lawrence County began in 1860. Since then, stone from the area has been used to construct such notable buildings as Washington, D.C.'s Pentagon and Department of Commerce building, and New York City's Empire State Building.

The engaging designs of the
actual Adena-Hopewell mounds
have been reproduced faithfully
in this piece.

MADISON COUNTY

Organized: 1823
Named for: James Madison
Major cities and towns: Anderson, Elwood, Alexandria, Pendleton

■ Curious raised shapes dot the landscape near a flowing river, as colorful, reflective feathers decorate the scene. Bordered by the White River, Madison County's Mounds State Park is home to ten unique earthworks constructed by the Adena-Hopewell people, a prehistoric group of Native Americans. The region also boasts a formidable automotive heritage. Between 1898 and 1920, nearly two dozen makes of automobiles—including the Lambert and Nyberg—were manufactured in the county seat of Anderson, and such auto parts manufacturers as Delco-Remy and Delphi Energy & Engine still call the area home.

LARAMORE.

48

MATERIALS USED:
Limestone, Plastic

ARTIST'S NOTES

Indianapolis landmarks visible in the Marion County piece include the Indianapolis Motor Speedway, the College Park "pyramids," the Lilly pharmaceutical factory, the state capitol building and the Indiana State Museum itself.

MARION COUNTY

Organized: 1822
Named for: Francis Marion
Major cities and towns: Indianapolis, Lawrence, Beech Grove, Speedway

■ Surrounded by a geometrical grid of colored squares, a gleaming white sparkplug stands proudly. In 1820, the Indiana Legislature began seeking a permanent location for the state's capital. After a centrally located site was chosen, in what is now Marion County, surveyors Alexander Ralston and Elias P. Fordham began platting the city of Indianapolis in 1821. Ralston had previously assisted Pierre L'Enfant in the surveying of Washington, D.C., and his Indianapolis plat incorporated elements of Washington's. Four years later, in 1825, the capital of Indiana was officially moved north from Corydon. Two of Indianapolis' better-known landmarks are the Soldiers and Sailors Monument at the city's center, and the Indianapolis Motor Speedway, a track in the town of Speedway that has hosted the Indianapolis 500 auto race since 1911.

Jemerson

49

The original plat map for Indianapolis is etched on the headstone of city surveyor Alexander Ralston, who is buried in Marion County's Crown Hill Cemetery.

Colored glass marbles were used to represent Marshall County's blueberries.

MARSHALL COUNTY

Organized: 1836
Named for: John Marshall
Major cities and towns: Plymouth, Bremen, Bourbon, Argos, Culver

■ In this decidedly cerulean piece, multitudes of blue spheres spring forth from the waters of a vast lake. Home to Lake Maxinkuckee, the second largest natural lake in Indiana, Marshall County also produces about one-third of all blueberries grown in the state. Justifiably proud of this fact, the town of Plymouth has hosted a Blueberry Festival each summer since 1966.

Jemerson

The Culver Military Academy, one of the United States' leading preparatory schools, has been located on the shores of Lake Maxinkuckee since its founding by Henry Harrison Culver in 1894. The school's many alumni include New York Yankees owner George Steinbrenner, who graduated from the academy in 1948.

ARTIST'S NOTES

The chrome-coated bronze in Martin County's piece reflects the blue of Indiana's skies and seems to ripple like water as visitors pass by.

MARTIN COUNTY

Organized: 1820
Named for: John T. Martin
Major cities and towns: Loogootee, Shoals, Crane

■ Layer upon layer of vertical strata is split by a glittering stream, tumbling from above. Gypsum, used to manufacture drywall and other building materials, has been mined in Martin County for years, and this piece makes use of actual cast acrylic gypsum. The region also is known for the natural beauty of Hindostan Falls, near the county seat of Shoals.

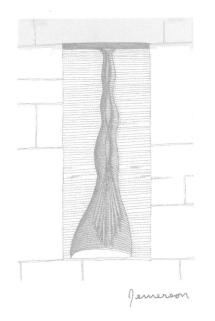

MATERIALS USED:
Cast Acrylic Gypsum (Forton®), Cast Silicon Bronze with Chrome Plating

Miami County's piece is a series of tangent arcs, representing the perfect symmetry of Cole Porter's cosmopolitan lyrics.

MIAMI COUNTY

Organized: 1834
Named for: The Miami Tribe
Major cities and towns: Peru, Bunker Hill, Converse

■ Grasping the crossbar of a trapeze, a dapper, gleaming figure spreads his tuxedo tails and prepares to ascend. Miami County's piece—a transom over a door on the museum's north side—honors songwriter Cole Porter, author of such classic tunes as "Night and Day," "Anything Goes" and "You're the Top." Porter was born and reared in the Miami County town of Peru, a community that also served as the winter home to seven circuses (including those of Hagenbeck-Wallace and Sells-Floto) between 1884 and 1944. This distinction is still commemorated by the town's annual Peru Circus City Festival.

Jemerson

Peru also is the headquarters of the International Circus Hall of Fame, a museum that preserves posters, costumes, props and other relics from famous circus performers.

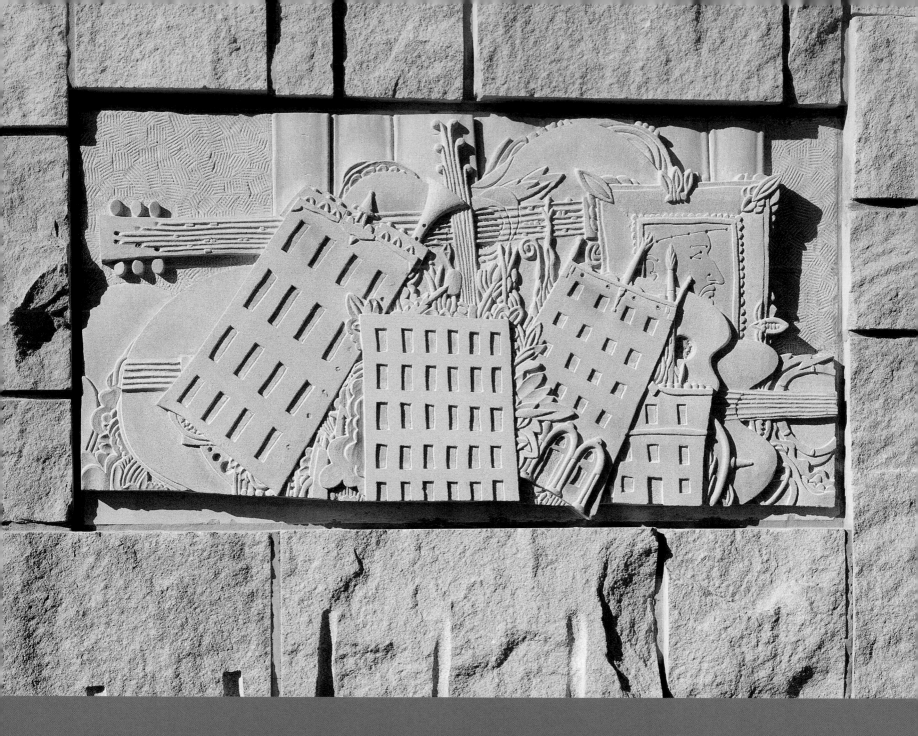

ARTIST'S NOTES

Master Stone Carver Mike Donham of Bloomington, Indiana helped to produce more than half of the 92 County Walk sculptures. The fabricator required a wide variety of carving tools to complete this piece, which demonstrates meticulous attention to detail in the lines of the buildings, the musical instruments—and Donham's own profile, concealed within a painting.

MONROE COUNTY

Organized: 1818
Named for: James Monroe
Major cities and towns: Bloomington, Ellettsville

■ Surrounded by music, art, theater and literature, a group of limestone buildings dance joyously, celebrating the rich cultural community that flourishes in the county seat of Bloomington. In addition to Bloomington, a city that has served Indiana as a center of education and culture for more than 150 years, Monroe County has been known since the 1800s for its limestone quarrying and stonecutting.

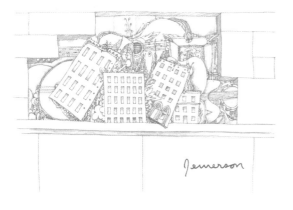

Monroe County's cultural heritage is amply represented by Hoagland "Hoagy" Carmichael, a Bloomington-born songwriter who led local collegiate jazz bands before penning the music for such classic melodies as "Stardust," "Heart and Soul" and "Georgia on My Mind."

ARTIST'S NOTES

The crest of the Roman helmet in Montgomery County's piece is formed by the rim and net of a bronze basketball hoop.

MONTGOMERY COUNTY

Organized: 1823
Named for: Richard Montgomery
Major cities and towns: Crawfordsville, Ladoga, Waynetown

■ Bronze leaves festoon a limestone basketball, creating the impression of an ancient Roman helmet. Lew Wallace moved to Crawfordsville, the seat of Montgomery County, in 1856, and authored his

best-selling novel *Ben Hur: A Tale of the Christ* in 1880. In 1892, Reverend Nicholas McKay introduced the one-year-old game of basketball to Indiana at Crawfordsville's YMCA. Years later, New Richmond, a small community in the northwest portion of the county, provided settings for the popular 1986 movie, *Hoosiers.* The region also possesses such recreational attractions as Sugar Creek, Lake Waveland and Shades State Park.

LARAMORE

In addition to being an author, Lew Wallace was a lawyer, diplomat and soldier. His services during the Civil War included organizing the defense of Cincinnati against Confederate forces from 1862 to 1863 and helping to prevent the capture of Washington, D.C. at 1864's Battle of Monocacy. After the Civil War, Wallace served as governor of the New Mexico Territory and U.S. minister to Turkey. Crawfordsville still honors his memory with the General Lew Wallace Study and Ben-Hur Museum.

ARTIST'S NOTES

The interconnected goldfish-like leaves in this piece were cut by laser from one single sheet of copper.

MORGAN COUNTY

Organized: 1829
Named for: Daniel Morgan
Major cities and towns: Martinsville, Mooresville, Brooklyn

■ In this piece, a tree-like school of goldfish (or, if one prefers, a goldfish-like tree) makes its way toward a far-off sun. Ozark Fisheries (formerly Grassyfork Fisheries, established in the Morgan County town of Martinsville in 1899) remains one of the world's largest goldfish hatcheries. The area also is home to the Morgan-Monroe State Forest, a wooded area that covers more than 24,000 acres of Morgan and neighboring Monroe County.

Morgan County residents Eugene and Max Shireman, burdened with farmland that was too swampy to be used for conventional farming, created Grassyfork Fisheries in 1899. Starting with 200 goldfish, the Shiremans eventually expanded their operation to encompass 1,500 acres and 600 ponds. Grassyfork was purchased by Ozark Fisheries in 1970.

ARTIST'S NOTES

The smaller figure in this art-work had to be created from the back of the larger, prompting the artist to refer to the pair as "Adam and Eve." The figures' heads are actual shattercone for-mations, retrieved from a stone quarry in Kentland.

NEWTON COUNTY

Organized: 1835
Named for: John Newton
Major cities and towns: Kentland, Morocco, Goodland, Brook

■ Two primitive figures nestle together, their nakedness covered by strategically placed mint leaves. In the Newton County city of Kentland lies a geological mystery known as the Kentland Dome. The presence of vertical strata and "shattercone" formations at the site cause many to believe that a meteorite may have plummeted to earth here, eons ago. The county's otherwise level land is used by farmers to grow a variety of crops, including peppermint and spearmint. Since 1965, the region also has harbored a prominent nudist resort in the town of Roselawn.

Jemerson

Shattercones are distinctive, cone-shaped rock formations, typically found in the stone beneath a meteorite's point of impact. It is estimated that the shattercones in Kentland were formed between 65 and 150 million years ago.

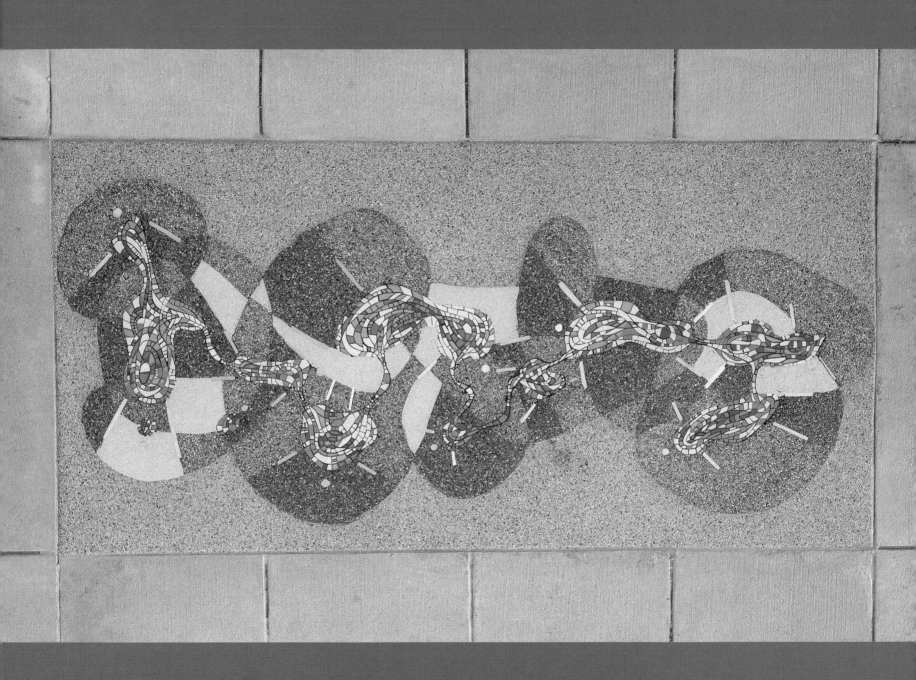

ARTIST'S NOTES

The horizontal plane of Noble County's lakes is echoed by the artwork's placement in the museum sidewalk.

NOBLE COUNTY

Organized: 1836
Named for: James Noble
Major cities and towns: Kendallville, Ligonier, Albion, Avilla, Rome City

■ A network of lakes winds its way through farmlands and forests, honoring the myriad, interconnected bodies of water in Noble County's Chain O' Lakes State Park. Located near the town of Albion, the park was opened in 1960, and today presents its visitors with the opportunity to fish, canoe, hike trails and otherwise relax on more than 2,500 acres of land.

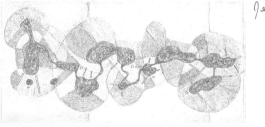

JAMES NOBLE

James Noble was a lawyer who settled in Brookville, Indiana, in the early 1800s. When Indiana became a state in 1816, Noble was elected to the U.S. Senate, where he served for 15 years until his death in 1831. His brother Noah was Indiana's governor between 1831 and 1837.

ARTIST'S NOTES

The top of Ohio County's piece has been slightly recessed, causing the stone of the museum's wall to resemble a wharf.

OHIO COUNTY

Organized: 1844
Named for: The Ohio River
Major cities and towns: Rising Sun

■ Viewed from above, a wheeled paddleboat steams away from port, ferrying its cargo to some distant location. The Ohio River forms the eastern boundary of Ohio County, the smallest of Indiana's 92. By the middle 1800s, the county seat of Rising Sun had become an expanding river town, recognized for its steamboat manufacturing.

LARAMORE

Reflecting Ohio County's boating heritage, the collection of Ohio County's Historical Society and Museum includes "Hoosier Boy," a famous 1920s racing boat designed by Rising Sun resident J. W. Whitlock.

ARTIST'S NOTES

The geode at the center of the Orange County piece was discovered by the artist himself, while touring southern Indiana.

ORANGE COUNTY

Organized: 1816
Named for: Orange County, North Carolina
Major cities and towns: Paoli, Orleans, French Lick, West Baden Springs

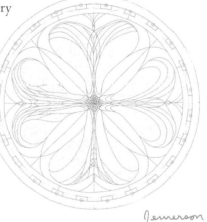

59

- From a center of crystalline shards, delicate white petals fan outward, forming a circular design that pays tribute to some of Orange County's more noteworthy attractions. The town of West Baden (adjacent to French Lick, birthplace of basketball legend Larry Bird) is home to the beautifully landscaped West Baden Springs Hotel, which once attracted thousands of visitors for its mineral baths and spa treatments. The hotel's lobby boasts a spectacular, unsupported dome measuring 200 feet in diameter, which was referred to as the "Eighth Wonder of the World" upon its construction in 1902.

- Orleans, the region's oldest town, is known for its flowering dogwood trees and was declared the Dogwood Capital of Indiana by the state's governor in 1970. Furthering the area's natural beauty, the area's riverbeds are excellent sources for the quartz-filled geological features known as geodes.

MATERIALS USED:
Granite, Gneiss, Geode

The outstretched figure of a woman is hidden within the flowing contours of the Owen County piece.

Owen County

OWEN COUNTY

Organized: 1819
Named for: Abraham Owen
Major cities and towns: Spencer, Gosport

■ Cascading gracefully to earth, this vertically flowing piece commemorates the natural beauty of Owen County. Near the village of Cataract, in the county's northern part, the laggard Mill Creek makes two abrupt plunges. When coupled with the cascades preceding them, the 20-foot upper falls and 18-foot lower falls add to a total drop of more than 80 feet. This elegantly simple piece, executed in blue cast glass, portrays Indiana's largest waterfall—Cataract Falls.

LARAMORE

60

The quiet splendor of Owen County also may be witnessed throughout the Lieber State Recreation Area, the Owen-Putnam State Forest and McCormick's Creek State Park, which was established as Indiana's first state park on July 4, 1916.

ARTIST'S NOTES

A swimming female figure is hidden in the flowing limestone waters of this piece.

PARKE COUNTY

Organized: 1821
Named for: Benjamin Parke
Major cities and towns: Rockville, Montezuma, Rosedale, Marshall

■ A cluster of roofed, pentagonal structures protrudes from a backdrop of rushing currents, honoring the many waters that course through Parke County, and the covered bridges that have spanned

them since the 1800s. Many pioneers entered this
region via the Wabash River, establishing mills along
Sugar Creek, Big Raccoon Creek and their branches.
Adding to the flow, the Wabash and Erie Canal—a
waterway that eventually stretched nearly 468 miles,
from Ohio's Lake Erie to Evansville's Pigeon Creek—

arrived here in the 1840s. Parke County has preserved a majority of its 19th century

covered bridges, 10 of which have now stood for more than a century.

BENJAMIN PARKE

*Lawyer Benjamin Parke came to the Indiana Territory around 1801, settling in Vincennes. He served
as attorney general of the Indiana Territory from 1804 to 1808, and as the area's first territorial
delegate to Congress from 1805 to 1808. Keenly interested in education, he was an early supporter of
Vincennes University, founded the state's law library, and organized the Indiana Historical Society.*

ARTIST'S NOTES

The Perry County piece offers a striking contrast between the hard lines of the sculpted lock and the flowing, organic shapes of the fish.

PERRY COUNTY

Organized: 1818
Named for: Oliver Hazard Perry
Major cities and towns: Tell City, Cannelton, Troy

■ Schooling fish wait patiently in two lock chambers, a salute to Perry County's natural and man-made phenomena. The Cannelton Locks and Dam project, constructed between 1963 and 1974, assists barges in their navigation of the Ohio River to the south. The region also is home to approximately 60,000 acres of the Hoosier National Forest, established by the U.S. Forest Service in the mid-1930s to preserve Indiana's open wilderness.

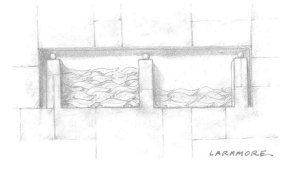

LARAMORE

Each time the Cannelton Locks are operated, 25 million gallons of water are required to raise or lower the water level by 25 feet.

In Pike County's representative artwork, the artist has created a striking contrast between positive and negative space.

PIKE COUNTY

Organized: 1817
Named for: Zebulon Pike
Major cities and towns: Petersburg, Winslow, Spurgeon

■ Traveling on an extensive network of tracks, loads of black cargo are ferried past gaping holes in an abstract composition of light and darkness. Since coal was discovered here circa 1860, the resource's mining and exporting has been an important industry in Pike County. Slightly north of county seat Petersburg, along the White River, two modern electric generating plants generate power for the rest of the state.

Jemerson

MATERIALS USED:
Limestone, Lead, Granite

ARTIST'S NOTES

The bronze grass atop the dune will, over time, gradually turn green.

PORTER COUNTY

Organized: 1836
Named for: David Porter
Major cities and towns: Portage, Valparaiso, Chesterton, Porter

■ Thick beach grass grows atop the crest of a grooved sand dune, reminiscent of the great hills of sand that border Lake Michigan in the region of Porter County. Indiana Dunes State Park was created here, in 1923. Expanded in 1966 by Indiana Dunes National Lakeshore, the area now provides a 14,200-acre preserve for more than 1,400 kinds of plants and animals. Many of Lake Michigan's beaches and dunes are part of this park system, offering crowds of visitors a welcome summer retreat.

LARAMORE

It was on the Indiana Dunes, at the turn of the last century, that University of Chicago botanist Dr. Henry Chandler Cowles conducted his landmark studies in plant ecology. Years later, Cowles was instrumental in the creation of Indiana Dunes State Park.

ARTIST'S NOTES

One of the red granite apples displays an evident bite mark.

POSEY COUNTY

Organized: 1814
Named for: Thomas Posey
Major cities and towns: Mount Vernon, Poseyville, New Harmony

■ An abstract, robed figure stands at the entrance to an intricate, apple-filled labyrinth, the center of which is occupied by a single, broken shackle. Posey County has been the site of two communal, utopian communities. In 1814, German leader George Rapp and his Harmonists arrived in the area and established the town of Harmonie, where they constructed a winding hedge maze (symbolic of the difficult path to true harmony) and prepared for Christ's second coming. Welsh-born industrialist Robert Owen purchased the town in 1825, renaming it New Harmony and bringing scientific and cultural leaders to the region to create a more perfect earthly society. The New Harmony labyrinth and several other properties are now Indiana state historic sites.

Jemerson

The broken shackle at the maze's center represents a letter written in 1862 by Robert Owen's oldest son, Robert Dale Owen, to President Abraham Lincoln, urging him to abolish slavery. Lincoln received Owen's letter on September 19, 1862 and three days later read a draft of his own Emancipation Proclamation to his cabinet.

ARTIST'S NOTES

The sandhill crane on the shield
is a whimsical substitute for the
Crowned White Eagle, a symbol
displayed on Poland's coat of
arms for more than seven centuries.

PULASKI COUNTY

Organized: 1839
Named for: Casimir Pulaski
Major cities and towns: Winamac, Francesville, Medaryville

■ Like rural heraldry, a regal bronze shield displays a strikingly bird-like ear of corn. Pulaski County—named for a Polish count who became a hero in the American Revolution—is home to rich farmland nourished by the Tippecanoe River. The Tippecanoe also flows near the Jasper-Pulaski Fish and Wildlife Area, an 8,022-acre property that attracts thousands of migrating sandhill cranes to the region each year.

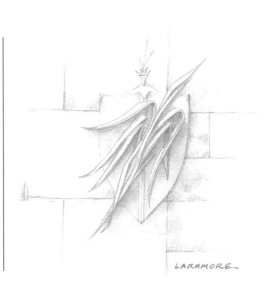

LARAMORE

Acquisition of land for what eventually became the Jasper-Pulaski Fish and Wildlife Area began in 1929.

ARTIST'S NOTES

The design of the owl's head allows it to rotate 360 degrees, following the wind wherever it goes.

PUTNAM COUNTY

Organized: 1822
Named for: Israel Putnam
Major cities and towns: Greencastle, Cloverdale, Roachdale

■ A stylized blue heron soars on currents of air, as a great horned owl below alertly scans the horizon. Mounted high atop a corner of the museum roof, this piece pays homage to a growing 15,000-acre natural area along Big Walnut River's deep stream corridor. In addition to an abundance of wildlife, some of Indiana's largest trees may be found in the old growth forest of the 2,697-acre Big Walnut Nature Preserve.

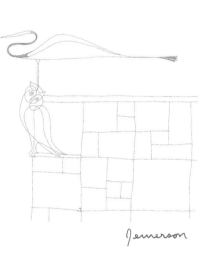

67

In 1968, the Big Walnut Creek was designated as a National Natural Landmark. The area includes eastern hemlock, Canada yew and other relict species of a post-glacial forest which occupied the area between 5,000 and 6,000 years ago.

ARTIST'S NOTES

Glass artist Fred DiFrenzi adeptly hand-blended various enamel colors, creating a marbled effect on this piece's surface. Gold leaf also has been applied, representing the scent of corn through pollen-like spots that waft above the tips of the stalks.

RANDOLPH COUNTY

Organized: 1818
Named for: Thomas Randolph
Major cities and towns: Winchester, Union City, Farmland, Parker City

■ From golden seeds, a network of roots grows to support towering, flourishing stalks of corn, the spiraling tassels of which resemble natural gas flames. Randolph County was settled largely by African Americans and Quaker farmers from the Carolinas, and the agricultural heritage they established continues today. The area also was home to glass manufacturers and related industries in the years following the state's 1880s gas boom, and Anchor Glass still maintains a plant in Winchester.

Jemerson

RIPLEY COUNTY

Organized: 1818
Named for: E. L. Wheelock Ripley
Major cities and towns: Batesville, Milan, Versailles, Osgood

■ Framed by handles along the sculpture's sides, a lithe human form stands outstretched atop a basketball-shaped temple roof. Ripley County—long known for its exceptional furniture, cabinet and casket-making industries—is home to Tyson United Methodist Church, which forms a distinctive part of the horizon in the town of Versailles. Basketball also looms large on this region's landscape, and the tiny town of Milan captured the state's imagination when the Milan Indians won the 1954 Indiana State High School Basketball Championship.

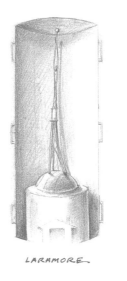

LARAMORE

Because its own gym was too small to accommodate fans, the Milan basketball team played its 1954 home games in the gymnasium of Versailles' South Ripley High School.

ARTIST'S NOTES

The artist considers this sculpture a tribute to "the magic that happens at fence rows."

RUSH COUNTY

Organized: 1822
Named for: Benjamin Rush
Major cities and towns: Rushville, Carthage, Glenwoods

■ The ragged geometry of a furrowed landscape is divided by bronze vegetation, a tribute to the fence rows that lure berries and birds alike to their boundaries. Thomas Jefferson's township grid, imposed on land north of the Ohio River by the Land Ordinance of 1785, divided the Indiana Territory into six-mile-square townships—which, in turn, were divided into smaller lots to attract westward-moving settlers. Homesteaders in Rush County were rewarded with some of the most productive farmland in the nation. Because this area once led the nation in pork production, the curving arc of a hog enclosure also may be glimpsed, contrasting with the hard angles that surround it.

Jemerson

Rush County's major agricultural products include corn, soybeans, wheat and alfalfa.

ARTIST'S NOTES

The "bullet-nose" design of the 1950 Studebaker's grill suggests the air intake of a jet aircraft. For this reason, the flowing limestone currents in this piece also may be interpreted as airflow.

ST. JOSEPH COUNTY

Organized: 1830
Named for: The St. Joseph River
Major cities and towns: South Bend, Mishawaka, Walkerton

■ A rushing current streams around objects in its path, creating the image of a classic automobile's grill. The Saint Joseph River—once traveled by Native Americans, French trappers, and American settlers—was in its last years as a significant form of transportation in 1852, when the H & C Studebaker blacksmith shop opened its doors in the city of South Bend. Changing its name to the Studebaker Manufacturing Company in 1868, the business soon became the world's largest manufacturer of horse-drawn wagons before switching to the production of gasoline-powered vehicles in 1904. The company continued to produce cars and trucks at its South Bend plant until December 1963.

LARAMORE.

The Studebaker National Museum, which displays more than 70 notable vehicles from the Studebaker Corporation's history, is located in downtown South Bend.

The Scott County piece was inspired by the contours of Hardy Lake, in which the artist saw the outline of a leaping bass.

SCOTT COUNTY

Organized: 1820
Named for: Charles Scott
Major cities and towns: Scottsburg, Austin

■ Against a wooded, cabin-filled background, a colorful largemouth bass leaps forward to engage a red, minnow-shaped lure. Scottsburg's Hardy Lake, a setting for fishing, swimming and other water sports, is a notable feature of Scott County—as is the region's land itself, which produces an abundant supply of tomatoes, corn, beans and other vegetables. In 1899, Joseph S. Morgan founded the Austin Canning Company in the town of Austin. Packing locally grown products, the business eventually became one of the nation's largest vegetable canneries, continuing today as Morgan Foods.

Jemerson

Hardy Lake is Indiana's smallest state-operated reservoir.

SHELBY COUNTY

Organized: 1822
Named for: Isaac Shelby
Major cities and towns: Shelbyville, Morristown, St. Paul

■ Bronze rails twine through book-like ties, creating a vertical track capped by the S key of a typewriter. In 1834, Indiana's first railroad opened in Shelbyville, county seat of Shelby County. Relying on horses to pull its wooden cars, the track covered just 1.25 miles, extending from the city's east side to picnic grounds on nearby Lewis Creek. Notable residents of Shelby County have included lawyer/writer Charles Major, who authored such popular novels as *When Knighthood Was in Flower* (1898) and *Bears of Blue River* (1901) and Sandy Allen, a 1973 graduate of Shelbyville High School who the *Guinness Book of World Records* has listed since 1976 as the world's tallest living woman.

LARAMORE.

The Bears of Blue River *was the first of three Charles Major books to be set on the banks of Indiana's Big Blue River. Subsequent volumes included* A Forest Hearth: A Romance of Indiana in the Thirties *and* Uncle Tom Andy Bill: A Story of Bears and Indian Treasure.

ARTIST'S NOTES

Lincoln—a modest, virtually egoless man—spoke much about others, but little about himself. Because his Hoosier heritage is seldom mentioned, the viewer must work to discover his image in this piece.

SPENCER COUNTY

Organized: 1818
Named for: Spier Spencer
Major cities and towns: Rockport, Santa Claus, Dale

■ A series of numbered limestone blocks build one upon another, forming the greater part of a man. In the fall of 1816, seven-year-old Abraham Lincoln moved with his family into what is now Spencer County, and settled into a community near the Little Pigeon Creek. He departed in March 1830, having just passed his 21st birthday. In the nearly 14 years that lay between, Lincoln once remarked, "I grew up." Reminders of Lincoln's past in the region include the Lincoln cabin site and the grave of his mother, Nancy Hanks Lincoln, both located within the boundaries of the Lincoln Boyhood National Memorial.

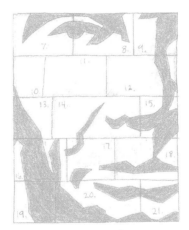

In Abraham Lincoln's **Autobiography,** *he notes that "Our new home was a wild region with many bears and other wild animals still in the woods."*

ARTIST'S NOTES

The figures of six family farmers may be seen in the lower right-hand corner of Starke County's piece.

STARKE COUNTY

Organized: 1850
Named for: John Stark
Major cities and towns: Knox, North Judson, Hamlet

■ Along both sides of a horizontal path, waters recede to reveal the emerging outlines of houses, barns and silos. Prior to the 1890s, Starke County was largely covered by swamps. Thanks to the development of drainage systems, however, much of the area had become usable, fertile farmland by the time the coast-to-coast Lincoln Highway arrived here in the early 1920s.

LARAMORE.

MATERIALS USED:
Limestone, Epoxy, Found Rocks

ARTIST'S NOTES

Exceptional work by Mark Parmenter at Spencer, Indiana's White River Foundry made it possible to cast Steuben County's thin bronze figures without exploding the mold—delicately preserving the designer's original vision.

STEUBEN COUNTY

Organized: 1837
Named for: Baron Friedrich Wilhelm Augustus von Steuben
Major cities and towns: Angola, Freemont, Hamilton

■ As control is abandoned, a lively tangle of human figures descends a steep slope as a single, inter-twined entity. Steuben County's 1,195-acre Pokagon State Park is best known for its 1,700-foot-long toboggan slide, a popular winter attraction. Throughout the other seasons, visitors may enjoy boating and fishing on nearby Lake James, or on one of the county's myriad other bodies of water.

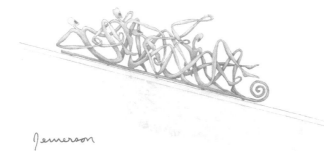

Jemerson

Pokagon's first toboggan run was built by the Civilian Conservation Corps in 1935.

ARTIST'S NOTES

*In this piece, the mined land of
Sullivan County is simply and
appropriately represented by a
recess in the rock itself.*

SULLIVAN COUNTY

Organized: 1817
Named for: Daniel Sullivan
Major cities and towns: Sullivan, Carlisle, Shelburn, Farmersburg

■ A blanket of new leaves grows thick, slowly covering man's presence. Coal has been mined in Sullivan County since 1816, and agriculture and coal continue to dominate the county's economy today. The Greene-Sullivan State Forest, which encompasses more than 100 man-made lakes and five campgrounds, is located on previously strip-mined land, as is Shakamak State Park, which was established here in 1929.

In 1918, when a mine operator planted 4,700 fruit trees along a mined area, Indiana became home to the first recorded instance of surface mining reclamation in the United States.

ARTIST'S NOTES

The curling tendrils of the grapevine conceal an understated human figure.

SWITZERLAND COUNTY

Organized: 1814
Named for: The country of Switzerland
Major cities and towns: Vevay, Patriot

■ On the page of an opened book, grape leaves vine up, around and through a decorated letter S—a tribute to Switzerland County's winemaking and literary heritages. In 1802, one of America's first commercial wineries was founded in this region by Swiss settler John James Dufour. Decades later, writer Edward Eggleston brought the region another kind of fame by authoring his best-selling 1871 novel, *The Hoosier Schoolmaster.* Eggleston's younger brother George, a lesser-known scribe, penned *Jack Shelby: A Story of the Indiana Backwoods* in 1906.

LARAMORE

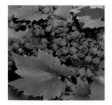

Every year, Switzerland County pays tribute to its past by holding a Swiss Wine Festival in the county seat of Vevay.

TIPPECANOE COUNTY

Organized: 1826
Named for: The Tippecanoe River
Major cities and towns: Lafayette, West Lafayette, Shadeland

■ Captured in a moment of deep loss, a despairing figure stands with arms extended. In 1808, Shawnee brothers Tecumseh and Tenskwatawa ("The Prophet") founded the village of Prophet's Town in what is today Tippecanoe County. The two hoped to join many Native American tribes into a united front and defend their lands against encroaching whites. Prophet's Town soon became the capital of an "Indian Confederacy," serving as a spiritual and physical training center for more than 1,000 warriors. Departing from Prophet's Town to recruit more allies, Tecumseh cautioned his brother to avoid battle during his absence. Tenskwatawa ignored him, and after the subsequent Battle of Tippecanoe on November 7, 1811, the United States Army—led by William Henry Harrison—destroyed Prophet's Town. Tecumseh returned several months later, learned of the battle, and realized that his dreams of unification were over.

79

A towering, 85-foot commemorative obelisk was erected at the battlefield's site in 1908. Today, Tippecanoe Battlefield, located seven miles north of the city of Lafayette, is a National Historic Landmark—home to an interpretive center that displays contemporary artifacts and includes an explanation of the battle from a Native American perspective.

ARTIST'S NOTES

The artist heated and flattened the bronze plant, making a sow's ear out of a tomato leaf.

TIPTON COUNTY

Organized: 1844
Named for: John Tipton
Major cities and towns: Tipton, Windfall City, Sharpsville

■ As a tomato vine curls upward, one of its larger fruits forms the face of a squinting, bronze-eared pig. Besides tomatoes, farmers in Tipton County produce dependably excellent crops of corn, soybeans and apples. Hogs, too, are a mainstay of this region and are celebrated by an annual Pork Festival in the county seat of Tipton.

LARAMORE

80

JOHN TIPTON

After John Tipton's family moved from Tennessee to Harrison County, Indiana, Tipton joined the Yellow Jackets, a band of local deputies organized by county sheriff Spier Spencer. A veteran of the Battle of Tippecanoe, Tipton served Indiana as a state legislator in 1819 and as a United States Senator from 1832 to 1839.

ARTIST'S NOTES

*The kayak in this piece is con-
structed from bronze, and the
kayaker himself is represented
by a small lead musket ball.*

UNION COUNTY

Organized: 1821
Named for: The Spirit of National Unity
Major cities and towns: Liberty, West College Corner

■ An intrepid kayaker makes his way through a rocky passage, paddling on a river of leaves. In 1949, Union County's Whitewater Memorial State Park was dedicated as a living memorial to the men and women who served in World War II. The 1,710-acre park's main attraction is a 200-acre man-made lake, on which no motorboats are allowed. South of the park, further recreation may be enjoyed on Brookville Lake, a 5,260-acre lake constructed between 1965 and 1974 on the east fork of the Whitewater River.

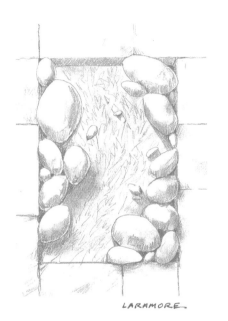

LARAMORE

MATERIALS USED:
Limestone, River Rocks, Lead Musket Ball, Bronze

ARTIST'S NOTES

The broken profile of the chieftain symbolizes a broken link with Angel Mounds' past, which has been partially reconstructed by archeological excavations.

VANDERBURGH COUNTY

Organized: 1818
Named for: Henry Vanderburgh
Major cities and towns: Evansville, Darmstadt

■ Feather and bead-like fragments crafted from aluminum lie buried in a ridge of stone, sketching an incomplete profile of a Native American chieftain. Angel Mounds State Historic Site, in the county seat of Evansville, is nationally recognized as one of the best-preserved prehistoric Native American sites in the United States. Beginning around the year 1100, the site was home to a Middle Mississippian Native American village, in which communal buildings were raised on large earthen mounds. According to archeologists, the town was mysteriously abandoned around 1450. Vanderburgh County also benefits from many industrial facilities in the area, including those of the Whirlpool Corporation, Mead Johnson Nutritionals and the Aluminum Company of America (ALCOA).

Jemerson

Angel Mounds is named after the family of Mathias Angel, an early white settler in Vanderburgh County whose farmstead stood on the site of Angel Mounds from 1852 until 1899. The land remained in the hands of the Angel family until 1938, when Indianapolis businessman Eli Lilly acquired the land to preserve it for future study.

ARTIST'S NOTES

Honoring Vermillion County's farming heritage, the typewriter has keys made of soybeans, as well as a corn-cob cartridge. Once transformed from paper, the river—like an actual current—gently carves its way into solid rock.

VERMILLION COUNTY

Organized: 1824
Named for: The Vermillion River
Major cities and towns: Clinton, Fairview Park, Cayuga, Dana

■ An endless sheet of paper rises upward from a simple typewriter carriage, transforming itself into a winding river as it ascends. In addition to its namesake Vermillion River, Vermillion County is bordered to the west by the Wabash River. The region's most notable citizen is likely Ernie Pyle, who was born near the town of Dana on August 3, 1900, and criss-crossed America from 1935 on, writing about the common people he met as a syndicated newspaper columnist. He marched with the armed services in World War II, where his simple, straightforward writing reported the war first-hand to millions of readers. He was killed by sniper fire near Okinawa, Japan in 1945. Pyle's boyhood home became a state historic site in July 1976.

LARAMORE.

Ernie Pyle once humorously suggested that a sign should be erected near Dana reading, "Three Miles South is the house in which E. Pyle, Indiana's great skunk-trapper, jelly-eater, horse-hater and snake-afraider-of, was born. In his later years Mr. Pyle rose to a state of national mediocrity as a letter-writer, a stayer in hotels, a talker to obscure people, and a driver from town to town."

ARTIST'S NOTES

This piece has been designed as a series of waves: horizontally in the flowing river, vertically in the swaying sycamores, and horizontally again in the blowing treetops.

VIGO COUNTY

Organized: 1818
Named for: Francis Vigo
Major cities and towns: Terre Haute, West Terre Haute, Seelyville

■ Song lyrics drift by in the waters of the Wabash, as the light of a stylized, rising moon gleams through sycamores on the riverbank. The Wabash River (and the National Road that later arrived here) made the Vigo County city of Terre Haute an early center of transportation. In 1897, Terre Haute-born songwriter Paul Dresser—assisted by his brother, author Theodore Dreiser—wrote "On the Banks of the Wabash," a best-selling tune that the 68th General Assembly adopted as Indiana's state song on March 14, 1913.

In addition to "On the Banks of the Wabash," other Paul Dresser compositions include "Just Tell Them That You Saw Me" (1895) and "My Gal Sal" (1905).

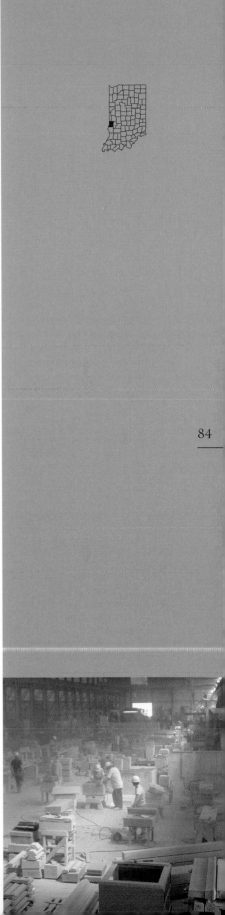

ARTIST'S NOTES

The flowing steel lines of the Wabash County piece were forged by an Indiana blacksmith.

WABASH COUNTY

Organized: 1835
Named for: The Wabash River
Major cities and towns: Wabash, North Manchester, La Fontaine

■ A graceful, aquatic structure stands alone, its curves glowing softly with electric light. Wabash County, named for the Wabash River that flows through it, is largely composed of farmland. However, at 8:00 PM on March 31, 1880, the county seat of Wabash achieved lasting fame when it became the first electrically lighted city in the world.

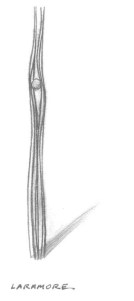

LARAMORE

The lights that initially lit the city of Wabash were four 3,000 candle-power Brush electric arc lamps, designed by the Brush Electric Light Company and installed on the courthouse tower. One of the lamps now rests in the courthouse foyer.

The subtle spirals of this sculpture were crafted from mild steel by ornamental blacksmith Jim Caldwell, of Martinsville, Indiana. From top to bottom, Warren County's piece measures 67 feet—the exact height of Williamsport Falls itself.

WARREN COUNTY

Organized: 1827
Named for: Joseph Warren
Major cities and towns: Williamsport, West Lebanon, Pine Village

■ Plummeting from the roof's edge, a tumbling stream of water atomizes into nothingness before reappearing as a crash of explosive spray. Formed by Fall Branch (a tributary of the Wabash River), Warren County's Williamsport Falls (located, naturally enough, in the town of Williamsport) descend 67 feet from an overhanging ledge to a rock-strewn ravine below.

Jemerson

The hook of the crane carries a seed, furthering its plant-like symbolism.

WARRICK COUNTY

Organized: 1813
Named for: Jacob Warrick
Major cities and towns: Boonville, Chandler, Newburgh, Lynnville

■ Rooted in coal, the derrick of a crane emerges from soil like a young plant, nourished by the rising sun. The land of Warrick County is rich in coal deposits, and mining has been an important industry here since the early 1800s. The region also is known for its production of corn, soybeans and other crops—much of it raised on farmland reclaimed from mining sites.

LARAMORE

It was around 1850, in the Warrick County town of Newburgh, that John Hutchinson sunk Indiana's first shaft for deep vein coal mining.

ARTIST'S NOTES

The number of holes in this piece corresponds to the actual number of identified caves and sinkholes in Washington County.

WASHINGTON COUNTY

Organized: 1814
Named for: George Washington
Major cities and towns: Salem, New Pekin, Campbellsburg

■ A series of craggy hills is pitted by dozens of small cavities, each one illuminated by the glow of a lamp. The beautiful, rolling and largely rural terrain of Washington County is recognized for its unusual number of caves and sinkholes. On July 10, 1863, the raiders of Confederate General John Hunt Morgan entered the county seat of Salem, cutting telegraph wires, burning bridges, ripping up the Monon railroad's tracks and extorting money from local merchants.

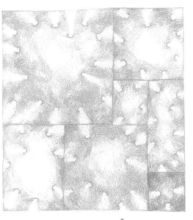

Jemerson

Caves of Washington County include Bat Cave, Dorseys Cave, Endless Cave, Flowstone Cave, Fredericksburg Cave, Frozen Waterfall Cave, Karens Pit Cave, Lamplighter Cave, Middle Cave, Mill Cave, River Cave, Trapper Cave, Waterfall Cave and the colorfully named Suicide Cave.

WAYNE COUNTY

Organized: 1811
Named for: Anthony Wayne
Major cities and towns: Richmond, Centerville, Cambridge City, Hagerstown, Fountain City

89

■ Resting atop a dotted highway, an artfully arranged stack of records forms the head and shoulders of a nurturing female figure. Established by an 1806 act of Congress, the National Road (America's first interstate highway) was constructed across Indiana between 1829 and 1834. A link between the eastern seashore and the country's western interior, the National Road was soon heavily traveled by westward-moving settlers—a migration honored by the Madonna of the Trail, an 18-feet-high monument in the county seat of Richmond. In 1915, Richmond's Starr Piano

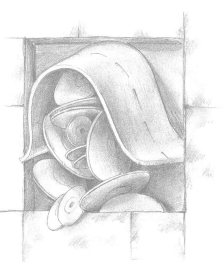

LARAMORE

Company entered the recording business. Changing its name to Gennett Records three years later, the adventurous label promptly began recording such seminal jazz artists as Jelly Roll Morton, Bix Beiderbecke and King Oliver's Creole Jazz Band, featuring a 21-year-old Louis Armstrong.

Richmond's Madonna of the Trail—located in the city's Glen Miller Park, and saluting "The Pioneer Mothers of the Covered Wagon Days"—is one of 12 such statues erected by the Daughters of the American Revolution. Wayne County's Madonna was dedicated on October 28, 1928 by future U.S. President Harry S. Truman.

ARTIST'S NOTES

A white marble at the tip of a feather symbolizes county namesake William Wells, a white man who lived for years as a Native American.

WELLS COUNTY

Organized: 1837
Named for: William Wells
Major cities and towns: Bluffton, Ossian, Zanesville, Markle

■ Captured in its youth, the slit of a germinating soybean resembles a white-tipped feather. The majority of this region's fertile land is used for farming, and local crops include soybeans, corn and wheat. The namesake of Wells County was William Wells, who was taken from his white family by Native Americans as a child. Though raised among the Miami, Wells later rejoined white society as a scout and interpreter.

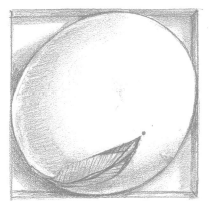

LARAMORE

90

WILLIAM WELLS

Taken from his natural family by Native Americans when he was 12 years old, William Wells was raised by the Miami and married Sweet Breeze, daughter of Chief Little Turtle. On November 3, 1791, Wells (named Apekonit or "Wild Potato" by his adoptive family) fought alongside Native Americans, defeating General Arthur St. Clair at Fort Recovery. Returning to white society shortly thereafter, Wells became a scout and interpreter for General Anthony Wayne. In the Battle of Fallen Timbers on August 20, 1794, he fought for the U.S. Army. He later settled in the vicinity of Fort Wayne with his Native American wife.

ARTIST'S NOTES

The sculpture's ski and tow rope form the point of an upward-directed arrow, symbolizing every skier's effort to ascend to the water's surface.

WHITE COUNTY

Organized: 1834
Named for: Isaac White
Major cities and towns: Monticello, Monon, Brookston, Wolcott

■ Balanced on one ski, an aspiring water skier gamely clutches a tow rope, his head creating a widening wake. The presence of Lake Shafer and Lake Freeman in White County has made this region a popular resort destination for Indiana and Illinois residents since the 1920s. Recreational activities in the region include boating, fishing, swimming and other water sports.

Jemerson

91

Lake Shafer was created by the 1923 construction of Norway Dam on the Tippecanoe River.
Similarly, Lake Freeman was formed by the construction of the Oakdale Dam on that same river.

ARTIST'S NOTES

The piece's cigar band, wrapping the ear of corn, also doubles as the clasp of a bassoon.

WHITLEY COUNTY

Organized: 1838
Named for: William Whitley
Major cities and towns: Columbia City, South Whitley, Churubusco, Larwill

■ Wrapped with a cigar band and capped by a feather-topped onion, a silo-like ear of corn displays joints reminiscent of a bassoon. Celebrated for its farming, this region was the home of Native American chief Me-Shin-Go-Me-Sia, or Little Turtle, born in 1782 near what is now the town of Churubusco. Whitley County also is the birthplace of Fox Products, a company founded in 1949 that fashions bassoons and such other double reed instruments as oboes, contrabassoons and English horns. Thomas Riley Marshall, Indiana's governor from 1909 to 1913, and U.S. vice president from 1913 to 1921, lived in county seat Columbia City from 1877 to 1909. Today, Marshall is best-remembered for his droll declaration, "What this country needs is a really good five cent cigar."

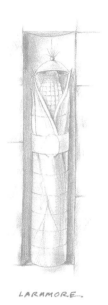

LARAMORE.

92

Upon leaving the office of U.S. vice president in 1921, Thomas Marshall was asked about his future plans. Marshall—a man of considerable wit—replied, "I don't want to work. I don't propose to work. I wouldn't mind being vice president again."

Canal

36

37 38 39 40 41 42 43

35

34   Dining

33   32   48   49   50

31

30

29

Canal Entrance   51 52 53 54 55 56 57 58

28

27
26
25
24
23
22
21
20
19
18   Washington Street Entrance
17   92 91 90 89
16
15

14 13 12 11 10 9 8 7 6 5

4   1

3

2

N

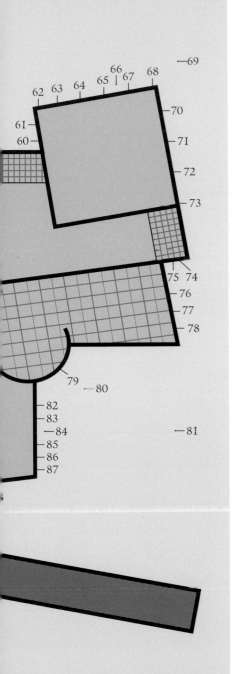

Adams	39	Hendricks	84	Pike	91
Allen	30	Henry	23	Porter	63
Bartholomew	48	Howard	87	Posey	80
Benton	31	Huntington	40	Pulaski	73
Blackford	77	Jackson	6	Putnam	28
Boone	16	Jasper	75	Randolph	47
Brown	86	Jay	11	Ripley	72
Carroll	70	Jefferson	60	Rush	57
Cass	25	Jennings	49	St. Joseph	18
Clark	3	Johnson	32	Scott	1
Clay	79	Knox	90	Shelby	41
Clinton	64	Kosciusko	82	Spencer	68
Crawford	78	LaGrange	5	Starke	56
Daviess	74	Lake	4	Steuben	42
Dearborn	52	LaPorte	44	Sullivan	61
Decatur	19	Lawrence	24	Switzerland	54
DeKalb	29	Madison	71	Tippecanoe	14
Delaware	20	Marion	45	Tipton	62
Dubois	17	Marshall	85	Union	88
Elkhart	43	Martin	9	Vanderburgh	22
Fayette	26	Miami	46	Vermillion	12
Floyd	59	Monroe	89	Vigo	34
Fountain	2	Montgomery	8	Wabash	69
Franklin	36	Morgan	55	Warren	7
Fulton	83	Newton	13	Warrick	58
Gibson	50	Noble	66	Washington	37
Grant	15	Ohio	27	Wayne	76
Greene	35	Orange	81	Wells	67
Hamilton	65	Owen	53	White	21
Hancock	33	Parke	38	Whitley	92
Harrison	51	Perry	10		

ACKNOWLEDGEMENTS

The Indiana State Museum and its 92 County Walk were created through the combined efforts of many hands and minds, but the project was led, steered and prodded by several key figures.

The Indiana State Office Building Commission—led by Executive Director Susan Williams, a former City-County Councilperson and history teacher—remained committed to the use of Indiana architects and artists throughout the project's construction. The organization's insistence that the building's exterior act as a teaching tool shaped the look of the project, and its unwavering leadership assured the museum's smooth, rapid progression from groundbreaking to completion.

Ratio Architects, Inc., founded on the belief that design should have purpose, was led by Principal Architect William Browne, Jr., AIA—pictured at left, with Susan Williams. Dedicated to excellence in architecture, interior design, historic preservation and landscape architecture, Ratio has changed the face of Indiana through such structures as Indiana University's Radio and Television Center (in Bloomington), the Emmis Communications World Headquarters (in Indianapolis), St. Bartholomew Roman Catholic Church (in Columbus) and many others. When called to define the look of the Indiana State Museum's exterior and interior, Ratio drew deeply upon all its skills. Showing great sensitivity to its site, the firm's striking, innovative design gracefully incorporated art into its architecture—and skillfully wove the threads of Indiana's 92 county histories into one compelling story.

In 1995, Indiana Governor Evan Bayh spurred the museum project by commissioning the construction of the IMAX Theater (later integrated into the museum building). Soon after, Governor Frank O'Bannon—pictured above at the museum's opening, between former governors Otis R. Bowen and Robert D. Orr—exercised considerable creative vision, made key decisions and (above all) consistently protected funding for the museum project, ensuring that the state's history would receive a unique, distinguished and honorable home.

MUSEUM PROJECT TEAM

Susan Williams, *Executive Director, Indiana State Office Building Commission*

Bob Wilson, *Deputy Director, Indiana State Office Building Commission*

Larry Macklin, *Director, Indiana Department of Natural Resources*

Jeff Myers, *Assistant Director for Operations, Indiana State Museum*

Jim May, *Manager of Collections, Indiana State Museum*

Kathleen McLary, *Vice President for Programs, Indiana State Museum*

Lee Alig, *Indiana State Museum Trustee*

Kent Agness, *Indiana State Museum Foundation*

Doug Wade, *Indiana State Museum Foundation*

Tom Castaldi, *Indiana State Museum Foundation*

Ron Newlin, *Executive Director, Indiana State Museum Foundation*

William Browne, Jr., *AIA, Principal, Ratio Architects*

John Klipsch, *Project Manager, Klipsch Consulting LLC*

Joyce Martin, *Office of the Governor*

RATIO ARCHITECTS, Designer

William Browne, Jr., *AIA, Principal Architect*

Rob Proctor, *Design Architect*

John Hartlep, *Project Director*

Bryan Strube, *Project Architect*

Brett Hatchett, *Project Architect*

Jennifer Broemel, *Project Architect*

Frank Rocchio, *Project Architect*

F.A. WILHELM, General Contractor

Christopher French, *Operations Manager*

Steve Ross, *Project Manager*

Doug May, *Project Superintendent*

Mike Wilhelm, *Masonry Contract Manager*

Scott Hesler, *Project Engineer*

Jason Whyde, *Installation*

EVANS LIMESTONE CO., Limestone Supplier

Steve Evans, *President*

Frank Ira, *Project Manager*

SPECIAL ACKNOWLEDGEMENTS

Governor Frank O'Bannon and First Lady Judy O'Bannon

Former Governor Robert Orr, *Indiana State Museum Foundation Board Member,* for his unwavering support of the Indiana State Museum

Generosity of Lilly Endowment

Community Foundations, County Commissioners and County Historical Societies, for their assistance in research

E.D. "Buck" Wilhite, Historian and aficionado of the places and spaces in Indiana

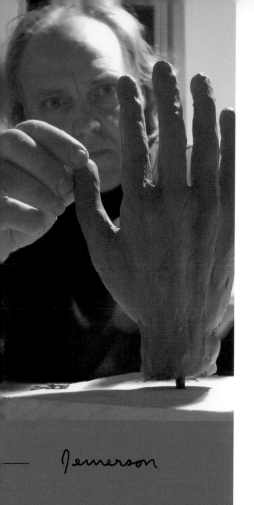

Jemerson

ACKNOWLEDGEMENTS

DAVID JEMERSON YOUNG   2nd Globe Sculptor/Design Principal

In addition to being an artist, writer and entrepreneur, David Jemerson Young—reared in Fountaintown and Indianapolis, Indiana, and educated in philosophy and literature at Indiana University—is a student of science, architecture and culture. As founder and design principal of 2nd Globe, Jemerson oversees the development of all projects.

Rather than specialize in one or two materials, Jemerson selects the media most appropriate for the project's site and subject. By himself and with others, he has pushed the limits of media with his approach, conceiving several innovative techniques.

Growing organically out of its purpose and environment, Jemerson's work discovers stories waiting to be told. The 92 County Walk project presented him with the opportunity to detect such stories time and time again. Jemerson's book of drawings, *Figures and Landscapes,* was published in 1996, and he has lectured and published widely on art, design and visual theory.

JEFF LARAMORE   2nd Globe Sculptor/Design Principal

An Indiana native with family roots in Knox and Middletown, Jeff Laramore holds a B.F.A. from Indianapolis' Herron School of Art, and began his career as an artist before becoming a nationally recognized, many-times-honored graphic designer. As a 2nd Globe design principal, Laramore has worked alongside Jemerson to develop the studio's singular approach to sculpture. Today, he has discovered his greatest gift, conceiving and developing astounding, award-winning artwork in three dimensions. A naturally objective observer, Laramore steers his prolific imagination in the exact direction a project should take. A precise eye, coupled with an exceptional aptitude for spatial planning, enables him to envision 2nd Globe sculptures during the design process and refine them before production. Laramore has worked in virtually all media, specifying materials according to the subject, site and conditions.

Laramore, especially noted for the superb craft of his compositions, expands his material vocabulary to fit his subjects. Throughout the creation of the 92 County Walk, that vocabulary was expanded considerably, as Laramore's artworks utilized an ever-growing array of different media.

2ND GLOBE

Based in Indianapolis, Indiana, 2nd Globe is an innovative company of visual storytellers. Meticulously researched and based on well-defined subjects, all 2nd Globe artworks contain multiple layers—creating engaging mysteries that stimulate viewers' imaginations.

Each 2nd Globe creation grows organically from its environment to communicate with audiences, raise questions and encourage dialogue—achieving a lasting fusion of beauty and artistic purpose. With the Indiana State Museum's 92 County Walk, 2nd Globe has created an enveloping, interactive, artistic and educational experience that assures visitors fresh rewards upon every new return.

XV

LARAMORE.

ACKNOWLEDGEMENTS

MATERIALS

Respecting Ratio's choice of architectural building materials, 2nd Globe artists Jemerson and Laramore made use of elements significant to Indiana's history, adding other complementary materials where appropriate. In all, more than 40 different materials were incorporated. Bronze, copper, glass and other substances were processed in several different ways, and many artworks combined two or more materials—adding to the pieces' range of contrasts, colors and textures.

After assembling a team of artists, artisans and fabricators, 2nd Globe's Jemerson and Laramore oversaw the production of each art piece, directing and supervising the works' developmental process from conception through installation.

Far more than simple executors, the members of this fabrication team used their own talents to further 2nd Globe's designs, pushing and often surpassing their own limits and those of their media. Time and again, the 92 county sculptures were dramatically enhanced by this collaborative process.

The Indiana State Museum, its foundation and 2nd Globe wish to recognize the exceptional work of David Bellamy, Alex Black, Jim Caldwell, Fred DiFrenzi, Mike Donham, Todd Ketchum, Rob Miller, Mark Parmenter and others, who helped turn design into tangible, admirable reality.

Clare Fox Acheson, Fox Studios,
Glass Artist *(Jay)*

David Kirby Bellamy,
Metal Sculptor *(Allen, Brown, Decatur, Fulton, Howard, Jasper, Lawrence, Pulaski, Ripley)*

Sarah Bellamy, The Projects,
Found Objects Artist *(LaGrange)*

Ron Beltz, JIT Waterjet /Classic Glass Company,
Custom Precision Waterjet Services *(Daviess)*

Alex Black, Alex Black Design,
Metal Sculptor *(Delaware, Fountain, Bartholomew, Boone, Clinton, Crawford, Dearborn, Franklin, Henry, LaPorte, Pike, Rush, Shelby, Starke, Vanderburgh, Whitley)*

Jim Caldwell, Narrowhaven Development Corp.,
Ornamental Blacksmith *(Warren, Tipton, Wabash)*

Ned Cunningham, Bybee Stone,
Stone Carver *(LaGrange)*

Jim Davis, Marvin Porter, Jamie Crawford, Paws Inc.,
Designer, Product Developer & Sculptor *(Delaware)*

Mike Donham, Accent Limestone Co., (formerly of Bybee Stone) Master Stone Carver *(Bartholomew, Blackford, Boone, Brown, Carroll, Cass, Clinton, Crawford, Dearborn, Dubois, Fayette, Grant, Greene, Harrison, Henry, Howard, Huntington, Jackson, Jefferson, Jennings, Knox, Kosciusko, Lake, LaPorte, Madison, Marshall, Monroe, Montgomery, Ohio, Parke, Perry, Pike, Porter, Ripley, Rush, St. Joseph, Scott, Shelby, Spencer, Starke, Sullivan, Switzerland, Tippecanoe, Tipton, Union, Vanderburgh, Vermillion, Vigo, Warrick, Washington, Wells, White, Whitley)*

Fred DiFrenzi, Vitramax Group Inc.,
Glass Artist *(Blackford, Floyd, Owen, Randolph)*

Ed Francis, Glass Artist *(Allen, Wabash)*

Tim Hildebrandt, Artist and Fabricator *(Greene, Jefferson, Kosciusko, Marshall, Martin, Miami, Montgomery, Parke, Tippecanoe, Union, White)*

Kevin Leslie, Metal Sculptor *(Gibson)*

Josh McCormick, Glasstrology,
Glass Artist *(Fountain, Marion)*

Rob Miller, Indiana Fan and Fabrication,
Mechanical Designer *(Clarke, Hancock, LaGrange, Marion, Miami, Morgan, Wayne)*

Mark Parmenter, White River Foundry *(Carroll, DeKalb, Elkhart, Johnson, Kosciusko, Martin, Miami, Montgomery, Newton, Parke, Scott, Steuben, Tippecanoe, Wells)*

Mark Richardson, Herron School of Art,
Ceramic Artist *(Clay)*

David Santarossa, Todd Ketchum, Santarossa Mosaic & Tile Co. Inc, Terrazzo *(Hancock, Hendricks, Noble, Posey)*

Dane Sauer,
Metal Sculptor *(Adams, Benton, Steuben)*

Donn R. Smith,
Commercial Sculptor *(Delaware)*

Bob Sorrels, Renaissance Woodwork,
Artist *(Dearborn, Pike, Shelby)*

Richard Ward, Keith Holshausen, Wardjet,
Waterjet Services *(Floyd, Marion, Noble, Orange)*

Michael Wilken,
Artist and Fabricator *(Wayne)*

Witt Galvanizing *(Warren)*

Mike Zapp, F.A. Wilhelm Construction Company,
Stone Carver *(DeKalb, Newton)*

2nd Globe Project Team
David Jemerson Young, Design Principal/Sculptor
Jeff Laramore, Design Principal/Sculptor
Paul Knapp, President
John Brooks, Production Manager
Meg Petersen King, Project Manager
Malissa Stafford, Project Manager
Courtney Rocchio, Project Assistant

ACKNOWLEDGEMENTS

ARTWORK SPONSORS: The Indiana State Museum Foundation thanks the following individuals and organizations, all of which (as of this book's first printing) have graciously and generously underwritten art pieces in the 92 County Walk.

The Hamilton-McMaken Trust (Allen)
Rick and Wendy Schrimper family (Brown)
The Dean V. Kruse Foundation (DeKalb)
Martha Bolyard (Elkhart)
James and Lalla Heyde family (Fulton)
Emily, Stephen, and Phyllis West (Gibson)
Robert Miles and Esther Miles (Greene)
Katz Sapper & Miller (Hamilton)
Santarossa Mosaic & Tile Company (Hancock)

McCormick Family Foundation (Knox)
Robert J. Hiler, Jr. (LaPorte)
Jack and Virginia Selig and Larry and Adrian Selig (Marion)
Mr. and Mrs. Dennis Faulkenberg & family (Perry)
Dr. and Mrs. Stephen K. Bailie (St. Joseph)
Friends of Starke County (Starke)
Centaur, Inc. (Tippecanoe)
Mothershead Foundation (Washington)
Anonymous (Ohio, Union, Warren)

BOOK DONORS: The Foundation also is grateful to Joseph F. Miller and Alice and Robert Schloss whose donations of funds have made the printing of this book possible.

GARRY CHILLUFFO: Photographer Garry Chilluffo, pictured at left, donated many extra hours of his time to create the full-page color photos of the 92 County Walk artworks that appear in this book. Born in New York State, Chilluffo attended the Rhode Island School of Photography and the Winona School of Professional Photography before moving to Indianapolis in 1976. Particularly noted for his architectural and advertising photography, Chilluffo has a strong personal interest in historic preservation.

PHOTO CREDITS:

The Foundation thanks all photographers, libraries and archivists who provided images for this book.

Indiana Department of Natural Resources
Photographers: Rich Fields, John Maxwell, Steve Polston: pg. III, VI, 1,15, 16, 19, 22, 24, 28, 36, 37, 46, 55, 60, 63, 64, 66, 67, 70, 76, 77, 78, 87, 89

Indiana State Museum building images, pg. IV, IX, XI,: ©Jeff Goldberg/Esto

Dan Patch, John Tipton, pg. 4, 80: Courtesy of the Indiana State Library

Joseph Daviess, pg. 14: Courtesy of the Galena Historical Society and Museum

Delaware Chief, pg. 18: Courtesy of the Ohio Historical Society

Lake Manitou Monster, pg. 25: Tippecanoe County Historical Association, Lafayette, Indiana Gift of Mrs. Cable Ball

Freewill Baptist Church, pg. 26: Courtesy of Josephine English Church and the Lyles Station Historic Preservation Corporation

James Whitcomb Riley, James Noble, Benjamin Parke, Thomas Marshall, pg. 30, 57, 61, 92: Courtesy of the Indiana Historical Society

William Hendricks and Jonathan Jennings, pg. 32, 40: Governors' Portraits Collection, Indiana Historical Bureau, State of Indiana

Elwood Haynes, pg. 34: Photo courtesy of The Elwood Haynes Museum

The Reuben Wells, pg. 39: Courtesy of The Jefferson County Historical Society

Culver Academy, pg. 50: Courtesy of the Culver Academy

Hagenbeck Wallace poster, pg. 52: Courtesy of the International Circus Hall of Fame

Hoagy Carmichael, pg. 53: Courtesy the Archives of Traditional Music, Indiana University, Bloomington, Indiana

Hoosier Boy, pg. 58: Courtesy of the Ohio County Historical Society, Rising Sun, Indiana

Cannelton Locks, pg. 62: Courtesy of US Army Corps of Engineers, Louisville District

Studebaker, pg. 71: From the collection of the Studebaker National Museum, South Bend, Indiana

Lincoln Cabin, pg. 74: Courtesy of the Lincoln Boyhood National Memorial

Washington County Cave, pg. 88: ©2003 Brian Killingbeck

William Wells, pg. 90: Allen County Public Library, Digital Photography Archive

BOOK CREDITS:

The book design, jacket design and text for *The Art of the 92 County Walk* were created by Young & Laramore Advertising.

Creative Direction: Carolyn Hadlock
Design: Pam Kelliher
Writing: Evan Finch
Project Supervision: Paul Knapp.
Malissa Stafford

Invaluable leadership was provided by the Indiana State Museum and other members of the book project team.

Susan Williams
Ron Newlin
Tony Nickoloff
William Browne, Jr.
Garry Chilluffo
Jessica DiSanto
Kathleen McLary

92

The body of this book was set in 11 point Centaur type, a serif roman face created by Bruce Rogers (a native of Linwood, Indiana and an 1890 graduate of Purdue University). Modeled after a 15th century font created by Nicolas Jenson, Centaur acquired its name from the book in which it made its first appearance, a 1915 Montague Press translation of Maurice De Guerin's *Le Centaure.*

The 204 pages were section sewn bound. The dust jacket was printed with four-color process and matte lamination, and the cloth cover includes a copper foil stamping.